WHO ARE THESE PEOPLE?

Always find humor
in life
Mariann

MARIANN CHAMBERS

This book is dedicated to my wonderful parents
Mary and Leonard.

ACKNOWLEDGEMENTS

My sincere appreciation and thanks to:

Laurie Rosin an amazing editor. Your insightful analysis transformed my words into something worth reading.

Rick Barry my copy editor for your attention to detail and words of encouragement.

Katherine at Kuszmaul Design & PR for your book cover and interior creativity, and help in navigating through the publishing process.

Miss Emma, Laura and Vivian for keeping my parents active and treating them with respect, kindness, and exceptional care.

Janet, Jan, and Peggy, good friends who shared their caregiver stories with me, and made me realize how universal caregiver experiences are.

Beth, Bill, Anna, and Don, wonderful friends who helped me care for Mary and Leonard when Jim and I traveled, and who listened to my countless caregiver stories.

My loving daughter Marisa, whose optimistic view of life, sensible advice, and assistance in caregiving helped me through many difficult times.

My best friend and loving husband Jim. Laurie Rosin is right, you are a saint. Without your support and encouragement I would never have achieved this goal.

PROLOGUE

One day while driving my parents home from their doctor's office, it suddenly occurred to me that I had spent the last three hours with strangers.

I had known and loved them as Mom and Dad, but somehow everything was different.

My mother had spent the last two years fighting dementia, and my father recently was diagnosed with dementia. On the outside they were the same, but inside a transformation was occurring, and I had no control over the outcome.

I too was experiencing a transformation. I could not stop their decline or mine.

They looked the same, but their actions were foreign to me. All I could do was wish and pray that my parents would return and these aliens would go back home.

I wasn't sure when it happened, but one day I was raising my parents. I was the one in charge-the one who had to make all the decisions, the one who managed the finances, and the one who worried.

I was taught from an early age to have deep respect and love for the elderly, so it seemed right that the responsibility of caring for my parents became my role. I was now a caregiver. This was a role I never aspired to obtain, tried out for, or expected to get.

I thought I was emotionally strong enough to handle the job, but it was much harder than I ever anticipated.

I decided viewing the situation with a sense of humor and a positive attitude would be the best direction to take for me, my husband, and the rest of the family.

The decision to document the experience was an effort to relieve my stress. After sharing my stories with friends and family, they encouraged me to publish a book in hopes it might be helpful for other caregivers.

CHAPTER 1
THE MIRACLE

MARY AND LEONARD

It all began in 2007. My parents were living alone in the two-family Victorian home my grandparents bought eighty-two years ago. Mom and Dad had lived happily in the house for fifty-eight and a half of their fifty-nine years together. Mom never wanted to move nor had the desire to live anyplace else. Dad was also very happy and content living there. Growing up, Mom, Dad, my brother Lenny and I lived on the second floor; grandma and Uncle Joe, Mom's mother and youngest brother lived on the first floor. The house was not large in size but was gigantic in the love, fun, and memories it held over all those years.

Mary and Leonard grew up a block apart in the same neighborhood and were both first-generation Americans born to Italian immigrants. They knew each other from childhood.

Dad was a friend of my mother's brother, and Mom a friend of my father's sister. Mom and Dad were friends, but never in a romantic way.

The spark came one day years later, when Leonard saw Mary in her bright-red winter coat. He was proudly wearing his U.S. Marine

Corps uniform. They were married in 1949, and had been insepa-
rable ever since. One was the other's shadow.

Mary graduated from Larson College which was taken over by Quinnipiac University, and worked as a manager for an insurance company until she had me. Three years later my brother Lenny was born. She performed her job as mother and wife to perfection.

Mary was not only our mother but the source of our life lessons. I still could recall her words as we left the house for school each day.

"Don't forget, no one is better than you are, and you can do anything you set your mind to. I love you. You make me proud."

Such a small thing, but her words had such a big impact on my
life. I learned to set goals and achieve them. Mom instilled in me a
lasting confidence.

Mary also taught us to be thankful. She walked into the kitch-
en every morning, and the first words out of her mouth were, "Thank
you God for this beautiful day."

One particular stormy morning stood out in my memory. I
questioned Mom on why she was thanking God for such a miserable
day.

She answered simply, "Any day I can get up and out of bed on
my own is a beautiful day."

Once while visiting Jim and me in Georgia, we drove Mom to see her best friend from grammar school. Peggy married a military man, and moved to Georgia years ago.

Peggy and Mom were ecstatic to see each other. They talked for hours. Peggy shared a story about my mother that described her perfectly.

Peggy had a rough childhood. Her father was an alcoholic, and her mother worked long hours to make ends meet.

Mom and Peggy met every day, halfway between their houses. Winters in Connecticut were cold and often snowy. Peggy's mom could not afford to buy Peggy gloves. Peggy shared with me my mother's solution. Mom gave Peggy her left glove and kept the right one.

Mom told her, "We can each wear one glove and carry our books in that hand, and put the other hand in our pocket. Now, we'll both be warm."

Mom was outgoing, friendly, kind-hearted, and always smiling. She had a great sense of humor and a quick wit.

Leonard graduated with honors from Boardman Trade School, and immediately was hired in the Design Engineering Department of the Winchester Repeating Arms Company a division of Olin Industries.

He believed every boy should join the military, and he served in the National Guard from 1938 until 1940. In 1942, Leonard proudly enlisted in the U.S. Marine Corps and served until the end of 1945. He smiled when he recounted to my brother and me how he stood on his toes to pass the height test; Leonard barely reached five feet, six inches.

His mother ensured him he would return safely from the war because he had been born with a veil of protection. The veil was the caul or part of the placenta covering his face at birth. It didn't matter whether Dad believed this was an old wives tale, superstition, or a gift from God bringing good luck. What did matter was that these were some of the last words his mother told him before she died.

Dad never talked about hazing at boot camp, crossing the equator, visiting exotic islands or anything about his South Pacific Marine experience.

My brother and I did remember one story that was passed on by our mother. Dad had just boarded a landing ship, tank (LST) leaving for battle. He was called off the ship because the replacement generator operator was delayed, and dad was the only one experienced enough to run the equipment.

In the end, his veil protected him. Most of his fellow Marines were killed in battle. From what I could piece together, this occurred during the Battle of Tarawa. Dad never discussed the war, and never left the house without his U.S. Marine Corps WWII veteran's cap.

After the war, Dad wanted to attend art school, but instead went back to work at Olin to help support his family. He accepted early retirement from Olin after thirty-eight years of service. At fifty-five he believed he was too young to retire, and was hired by Dresser Industries where he worked until he retired at sixty-five.

Leonard was a perfectionist, a hard worker, quiet, and described by everyone that knew him as a nice guy.

My parents spent the years after Dad's retirement involved with local senior clubs, their church, and their grandchildren.

Mary and Leonard were great parents. As a family, we ate dinner together every night, and attended church together every Sunday morning. Mom and Dad provided my brother and me with the best private education they could afford, even at the expense of doing without for themselves. They gave us discipline, guidance, encouragement, and unlimited love.

TIME TO LEAVE (2/11/2007)

In 2007 Dad was eighty-six. The extent of his driving was to the grocery store, church, the senior-citizen clubs, and their various medical doctors. Since they lived in the city, none of these trips required long-distance driving. Dad was beginning to forget the directions to many of their doctors' offices, which concerned me. He would joke about the lapses in memory. "We made it home today, so I guess we still recognize some of the streets."

My husband Jim and I had moved to Georgia twenty years earlier and recently retired in Savannah. Jim's daughter JoAnn, son-in-law Tom, and two grandchildren, T.J. and Katie, lived fifteen minutes from my parents, so visits to Connecticut were frequent.

Whenever we visited my parents, I would wimp out and ask my husband to go to the store with Dad and check out his driving. Jim would come back laughing. He'd report, "Leonard is doing fine, and he knows every stop sign he can go through."

Jim proceeded to explain that while driving through the neighborhood, my Dad rolled through many four-way stop signs. When Jim questioned him while they were driving, Dad replied, "I've lived here my entire life, and no one ever goes down this street, so I don't have to stop."

I didn't find this as humorous as Jim.

Dad was smart enough to know his limitations and would take Mom grocery shopping on Sunday mornings when everyone else was in church. He and my mother would go to church on Saturday night. Their church was two blocks from home.

Dad was also having a difficult time getting in and out of his 2000 white Toyota Camry. The car was always parked on the street in front of their house. He would sit sideways facing the street, and as the traffic whipped by he proceeded to lift his right leg into the car and repeat the process with his left leg while turning his body to face forward. It was a slow process. Watching him get in and out of the car was painful, and scary. Their desire to remain independent was strong. My desire to keep them independent was equally strong, but I was beginning to fear the consequences of his driving.

Mom had never learned to drive. She enjoyed repeating the story of her one attempt.

"Your Dad took me out one Sunday to teach me how to drive. I still remember him yelling at me. He would yell, 'You're too close to the curb and going to ruin my white-wall tires.' I told him I was not going to learn, and he would have to chauffeur me around forever, and he has."

Mom never liked to cook but until this year prepared great meals with fresh vegetables and dessert. She believed fresh broccoli was the secret to longevity and served it at every meal. Dad was not big on eating vegetables and would eat the broccoli first in a very medicinal manner.

Recently, it seemed that Mom at eighty-four considered hot dogs her favorite gourmet meal which she served several times a week. When questioned about her new diet, she replied:

"Your Dad loves hot dogs, and I'm getting tired of cooking."

Mom and Dad still lived on the second floor of their two-family home, despite my attempts to get them to move downstairs. Throughout the years, they were fortunate to have rented the first floor to wonderful Yale graduate students. These caring people often helped carry the groceries up to the second floor. This had become a tiring task for my parents. In return, my parents would buy extra orange juice, bananas, cookies, ice cream, or some other treat to share with their tenants. Even after the students moved, they would send Mom and Dad postcards, letters and Christmas cards.

During recent visits to Connecticut from my home in Georgia, I had begun to notice Mom was getting lax in her housekeeping. She took great offense when I asked if she would like a cleaning lady to help with the housework.

"Are you telling me my house is dirty?" she asked.

My comments about getting a cleaning person bothered her for weeks, and every time we spoke she asked me if I thought her house was dirty.

I called my parents at least two or three times a day to check on them. This helped relieve my guilt and lessen the stress of worrying about them.

My brother, sister-in-law Marie and nephew Michael lived in New Jersey. They were a four-hour drive from Mom and Dad. My mother's brother Joe, and his wife Cathy, lived near my parents, as did several of my cousins, but Mom and Dad never wanted to be a burden on anyone and rarely asked for help.

Recently conversations with my mother increased my stress and worry levels. A typical conversation with Mom would go something like this:

"We went to the senior club today, and I won two dollars."

"That's great, Mom. Glad you had fun. How's the weather up there?"

"It was beautiful today. We went to club, and I won two dollars."

I didn't want to make her feel bad by telling her that she had already told me this.

"Great. Your winnings paid your club fee today."

"Yes. And tonight I am cooking hot dogs, beans, and of course, broccoli. Did I tell you we went to club, and I won two dollars?"

I almost cried. After several similar conversations, I tried to explain my mother's repetitive comments by telling myself she didn't have that much to talk about. In the pit of my stomach, I knew better. The time for them to leave their home was coming soon.

THE RAZOR BLADES (4/22/2007)

I made it a point to call Mom and Dad late Sunday morning to make sure they had returned safely from the grocery store.

This Sunday Mom's voice was shaky when she answered the phone.

They got into an accident, I thought. I took a deep breath before going on and prayed Dad had not injured anyone. I was upset with myself for not taking the car away from him sooner.

"Mom, is everything okay?"

"Everything is fine," she answered in a tone that scared me.

I never liked the use of the word fine to describe a good situation.

I kept probing. "Is Pop all right?"

"He's fine."

"Mom, I sense something is wrong. What happened?"

It was at this point that her voice changed to a whisper. "You have to promise not to tell anyone. Dad got in trouble."

"Please tell me what happened."

"Your father needed razor blades and went to look for them while I shopped. We checked out, and as we were walking out the door, an alarm went off, and the store security guard stopped us. The guard frisked your father and found a package of razor blades in his coat pocket. He said your Dad can never go back into the store, or they will arrest him."

I could not believe what I heard. "Did you ask Pop why he did it?"

"He doesn't remember putting them in his pocket."

My reaction was shock and disbelief. My father was an honest man and would never take something without paying. What was happening to him?

From that day on, Dad waited in the car while Mom did the shopping. I felt it unfair that the store wouldn't at least allow an eighty-five-year-old man to sit inside at the front of the store especially in the winter. My parents had been shopping there for years, and because Mom knew where to find every item, refused to shop elsewhere. I advocated that I call the manager, but this upset both of them. So, poor Dad had to wait outside in the car.

HAPPY BIRTHDAY (9/8/2007)

The summer passed without any issues, and mom's memory appeared stable. In September, Jim and I ventured to Connecticut to pick up my parents and bring them to Charleston, South Carolina. My daughter Marisa and son-in-law Ricardo were planning a party to celebrate their daughter Isabella's first birthday. My granddaughter was blessed to have been born on the same day as her great-grandmother. I didn't want my parents to miss her first birthday party. We had a wonderful celebration, and Mom was so pleased.

The next day, I mentioned how beautiful the day was and how nice it was to have two birthday celebrations and two cakes.

Mom replied, "I didn't have a birthday party or cake."

Forgetting a cake was no big deal but forgetting that more than twenty people sang "Happy Birthday" to you and shared your cake was.

The day after Mom's birthday, Marisa, who was a clinical psychologist, gently suggested I take Mom to see a geriatric psychiatrist. She felt medication might improve or delay Mom's memory loss or at least help her cope with the problem.

I became a single mom when my daughter was a year old. The experience made me rely on my parents a great deal. They played a significant role in raising my daughter. After moving to Georgia my daughter and mother remained close.

The next day I spent hours on the phone and Internet, learning everything I could about memory loss and aging. The idea that my mother whom I viewed as intelligent and sharp may have dementia or worse was frightening. After numerous phone calls, a gentle-sounding doctor called me back and said he would be happy to meet with us.

I made the appointment for the week Jim and I took them back to their home in New Haven.

THE PSYCHIATRIST (10/31/2007)

Driving to the doctor's office, mom kept questioning me as to why she needed to see a doctor when nothing hurt.

I wished I could have removed the sign in the lobby that clearly spelled out *Psychiatrist*. I positioned myself slightly in front of her as we entered the elevator so she wouldn't see the sign. Since my mother stood about four feet, ten inches tall – she used to be five-foot-one – I easily blocked her view. But nothing could have covered the words on the doctor's office door. Mom's eyes grew big as she saw the words *Dr. Sho - psychiatrist*. She immediately began to yammer. "Not sure why I'm here. Do you think I'm crazy?"

"No, Mom, I think you're having a little problem with anxiety, and the doctor can help you with that."

"I have a little problem with my brain, and I'm not sure anyone can help with that," she sternly answered me.

This was the first time she acknowledged her memory problems. I was frightened to think what the future would hold for my parents, and I hoped the doctor would fix everything.

The doctor allowed me to stay in his office as he spoke to Mom, and would only let me respond to questions regarding her medical history. Mom attempted to answer all his questions, often looking toward me hoping I would provide the answers. He wanted to meet with Mom several more times in order to properly assess her condition.

I was able to accompany Mom on two other doctor visits, and my aunt and uncle took her to the other appointments.

On both occasions, the conversation as we walked into Dr. Sho's office was the same.

"What day is today? It's December, right? What did I have for dinner last night? Bush is the president. Who was the president before Bush?"

Mom tried to outsmart the doctor by remembering the questions he asked during prior visits.

After several visits and many tests, Dr. Sho informed me my mother was difficult to assess but was suffering from dementia. He explained the tests he had administered and described how Mom had had difficulty drawing a simple clock.

Mom was asked to draw a clock, put in all the numbers, and set the hands at a certain time.

The clock drawing test was a screening tool used to detect dementia. One point was given for correctly completing the tasks: drawing the clock circle, sequencing the numbers correctly, placing the numbers in the proper position, drawing two hands on the clock, and pointing the hands to the correct time. A normal score was between four and five. Mom had the numbers on the clock out of sequence and in the wrong places. She scored a three.

Dr. Sho told me her condition would worsen. Thankfully, he never mentioned the *A*-word. He advised me to move my parents closer to family within the next six-to-twelve months.

He handed me two prescriptions, one for Aricept used to treat mild to moderate dementia, and the other for Citalopram. He prescribed 10mg of Citalopram for Mom's anxiety and to avoid depression. The memory loss was causing Mom to be anxious.

Jim called this her "happy pill." I wasn't a proponent of medication, but this little pill had helped my mother cope with her problem without depression or anxiety. She was a happy person and the medication did not seem to change her personality.

There were days when Jim and I laughed and said to each other, "Do you think Mary would miss a pill or two?"

THE RIGHT DECISION (11/11/2007)

Jim and I decided only one option would work: move my parents closer to us. But how would we accomplish this miracle?

After much deliberation and prayer, I decided to use an honest and direct approach. I believed my parents were ready to move but didn't want to burden their children. They would never take the initiative and act on their own. I didn't ask them what they wanted to do. The answer to that question would have been, "Stay right where we are." I wanted to make them feel the decision was theirs and not take away any of their independence.

Taking the advice of my daughter, I used an approach she suggested parents use on their children. I gave my parents three options and left the decision up to them. I provided them with realistic solutions and made it clear that staying in their home alone was not an alternative. Before making a decision my mother said, "Well, I'm not sure I like any of these."

1) Hire a full-time, live-in caregiver.

2) Move to a retirement community in Connecticut not far from their current home.

3) Move to a retirement community in Savannah, Georgia, close to Jim and me.

They chose number three.

I knew how hard it was for them to accept that living alone was no longer an option, but I also knew I had to be firm.

Weeks after they agreed to move, I wondered if Jim and I had made the right decision. I felt I was taking away my parents' independence and was beginning to feel the guilt.

On several occasions my Uncle Joe expressed his concerns to me about them living alone, but even after the decision to move was made, I still worried about Mom and Dad leaving their home.

One night Mom informed me that a person from AARP was coming to visit them at nine o'clock the next morning to discuss their medical insurance.

"Who is coming to see you?" I questioned.

"Someone from the AARP."

All I could think of was that my parents were the targets of a scam. They might be robbed, or even worse, hurt in the process. My fear immediately turned to anger. Why would someone take advantage of my parents?

"Did they ask for any information over the phone like your social security number or bank account number?"

"No, and the lady sounded very nice."

"Mom, AARP doesn't send salespeople door to door. This might be a scam or someone trying to get in the house to rob you."

"Don't be silly." She said irritated.

"Did they give you a phone number?"

"No."

"Put Pop on the phone, too," I commanded.

I proceeded to explain why they shouldn't answer the door in the morning. Mom continued to tell me she could handle it and assured me I had nothing to worry about. I finally raised my voice and stated I was going to call my uncle or the police if they didn't agree to not answer the door. They finally agreed.

My mother had always been afraid to answer the door for anyone. She would never make an appointment with a stranger or let them come into the house. That woman I was speaking with was not acting like my mother.

I hung up and immediately called AARP. They confirmed they do not make house calls. They agreed it sounded like a scam and would report the incident to the police.

The next morning at eight-thirty, I called Mom and Dad. I could not believe what I was hearing. Mom started to tell me a person from AARP was going to be there at nine. I felt so frustrated. Didn't they understand what I explained to them yesterday? I stayed on the phone with them until nine-fifteen. No one ever came to the house, but at that point I knew Jim and I made the right decision. They could no longer live alone.

CHOOSING THEIR NEW HOME (12/7/2007)

I viewed choosing the right "home" for my parents as one of the most important decisions I had to make. I had heard many horror stories from friends about how unhappy their parents were after they moved from their homes.

Several years ago, while Mom and Dad were visiting Savannah, Jim and I decided to take them to see some retirement communities. Admittedly, I did not do my homework beforehand to understand the amenities retirement communities provide such as: meals, laundry facilities, medical services, transportation and social activities. I wrote down the addresses and off we went. I shortly found out this was a huge mistake.

Unlike some communities that house independent, assisted and nursing services at the same location, the first place on the list was a totally independent retirement residence. It took us ten minutes to get Mom out of the car.

"I don't want to move, and I don't want to live in a senior home. If you want to see this place for yourselves, go ahead. I'll wait in the car," she declared.

I was ready to scream, since we had discussed our plans for the day prior to leaving the house.

Jim saw the expression on my face and turned toward Mom. "Mary, we drove all the way here. Mariann is only thinking of your best interest. The least you can do is look at the place."

That did it, and Mom reluctantly got out of the car, cane in hand. Leonard holding his cane followed her lead. She and Dad went through the motions, were polite, but said very little as we toured the facility.

My next mistake was to take them to see a facility which housed both independent and assisted-living residents together. The residents were all very pleasant, but seeing some of these people in wheelchairs and lifeless did not leave any of us feeling good about the future.

Now that the situation had changed, and the decision made to move to Savannah, I thought my parents would be interested in making the selection. What I received was a negative reaction to choosing a new home.

After that, I knew the decision would be mine to make. My criteria for choosing a place for Mom and Dad consisted of two items: 1) A clean kitchen - I read somewhere if the kitchen was clean, the facility would be well run. 2) Smiling residents and staff - my daughter used this one when she was looking at colleges. If I were doing this again, I would add one more to my list: 3) Activities – I learned the importance of daily and diverse activities both on-site and off-site. An energetic activities director was an asset.

I found Savannah Seniors, an independent retirement community that met all of the important criteria, eight miles from my home. The kitchen was immaculate, the residents and staff were smiling and friendly, and a wonderful activities director was constantly finding interesting ways to keep the residents busy.

My parents were not ready for assisted living. They were able to manage day to day living without help. Savannah Seniors did provide limited assistance with the activities of daily living (ADL'S), if needed.

I put a deposit on an apartment with a good size living room, kitchenette, large bedroom, and another small room that ended up as storage for boxes of precious memories. That was the only apartment available, which I viewed as a positive sign.

THE CAR (1/24/2008)

We all knew Dad needed to end his driving career. What better way than with an unblemished driving record – except for the one time he hit a car full of nuns. Fortunately no one was hurt and very little damage was done to either car, but it is a story he loved to tell.

The white Toyota Camry was in relatively good shape except for the occasional scratch and a couple of small dents of unknown origin.

I read several suggestions on different websites as to how to get a parent to stop driving but none of the methods seemed right. I knew that often the only way was to take away their car keys, but it would be great if I could make my father feel the decision was his.

Then out of the blue it came to me: my nephew Michael was about to start law school and needed a car. How easy. I told Dad his grandson needed a car. Whenever he felt ready to stop driving, he could give the car to Michael.

Dad immediately picked up on my words. "I'll stop driving, so he can have my car."

He made the decision; I provided a good excuse. I think he knew he was ready, but wasn't sure how they would survive without transportation. So right after his eighty-seventh birthday, Dad gave up the car.

Family, friends and the local senior My Ride, a city-run transit program for seniors, provided transportation for my parents until they moved to Savannah. Both my parents seemed content with this situation.

OUR FAMILY HOME (3/30/2008 – 4/3/2008)

Jim and I spent a week dismantling the contents of a home that took fifty-eight years to accumulate. The scope of such a project was overwhelming. There were six rooms, an attic and full basement.

My brother's attachment to the house prevented him from agreeing to sell it to strangers. He bought it to use as rental property.

Lenny, Marie and Marisa offered to help, but I knew if we were all working together, the memories and stories would interfere with the job.

I arranged to have my parents out of the house, spending time saying good-bye to relatives and friends while we tackled the job.

I took a deep breath and started in the smallest closet. Completing one little step gave me the incentive to move on to bigger challenges.

In a larger closet, I found a heavy box covered in dust. Jim helped me get it down. We were both curious as to its contents. Inside the box were heavy, long, gray and burgundy draperies. They were dusty and discolored. We inspected the perfect and precise stitches my grandmother had sewn by hand to make what were at one time beautiful draperies. With reservation, I put them in the trash pile.

When Mom returned from the day's outing she saw the box. "What are you throwing out now?"

Before I could answer the box was open. "My mother made these. Can't you use them in your house?"

"Sorry, Mom, but these are too heavy for the South."

She made several other suggestions on how to reuse the draperies and finally accepted that they were part of the past that could not move forward.

Each day was spent putting things into large trash bags that were sorted into three piles: trash, Goodwill, and movers. Having a garage sale entered my mind, but required a level of effort and time that neither Jim nor I could devote.

Upon their return home each day, Mom would look confused and begin to open the bags, salvaging various items.

I decided tackling the contents of Mom's hope chest with her would be fun. When Mom was young, hope chests were used by women to store clothing and linens in anticipation of marriage. My parents used the chest as a table upon which sat their telephone and stereo. It was like opening a time capsule. The scent of cedar permeated the room. It contained a dozen unworn silky, "sexy" nightgowns and robes, probably wedding shower gifts from 1949. We carefully removed hand-crocheted doilies and cross-stitched aprons from the tissue paper that had kept them clean all these years. They were all lovingly made by my grandmother.

At the bottom of the chest was the best find of all, a full-size bedspread hand-crocheted by my grandmother. Mom didn't remember it. It was beautiful and must have taken my grandmother months or even years to make. My Mom wanted me to have it, but I felt after almost fifty-nine years, it should be on my parents' bed as originally intended.

The next room to tackle was the kitchen. Fortunately, Mom gave me a heads-up before cleaning out the cabinets.

"Don't throw any pans out until you look inside them. That's where my jewelry is hidden."

As warned, in every pot and pan was a small box containing a cherished piece of jewelry.

The biggest challenge was the attic, which I was certain they had not visited in years.

Growing up during the Depression gave my parents the right to save everything because "You never know when you might need it."

I had the most difficult time parting with the past in the attic. As a child, I remembered the attic being an exciting and mysterious place. The attic was a storage area for both junk and treasures.

If it weren't for my husband, who helped me sort through all the stuff, I would still be in that attic. It was an eclectic mix of old furniture, military uniforms, mementos, pictures, tools, clothes, toilet paper, canned food and liquor. Everything was wrapped in plastic bags or paper - my guess was to keep things clean.

Six boxes of liquor, each containing about a dozen bottles opened and unopened lay in a corner. My parents weren't big drinkers, so I was surprised to find all the alcohol. Then I realized where it came from, and Dad confirmed my assumption. Most of the bottles were bought thirty-six years before, for my first wedding.

Jim used the liquor as fertilizer for the grass and proceeded to pour out the contents of every opened bottle. I knew it was killing him to waste good liquor. He did manage to salvage several sealed bottles to take home.

As the week progressed, we arranged to rent a truck for hauling trash to the dump. More than sixty trash bags were marked for the dump. We had already made six trips to Goodwill.

Jim and I went to the local U-Haul office on a snowy day. I waited in the car as he went to rent a truck. He came back in a matter of minutes. "You need to sign for the truck," he announced.

"Why? You're driving."

"No, you're driving. My license expired," He answered sheepishly. Jim's birthday is in October, so he had been driving without a renewed license for five months.

I signed for a medium-sized panel truck and proceeded to climb into the driver's seat. As I went to adjust the rear view mirror, I found out there was none. Realizing I would have to depend on the side mirrors sent me into panic.

I glared at my husband. "No way am I driving this big thing in the snow without a rear-view mirror."

He went back inside and satisfied me by exchanging it for a small pickup truck.

To unload at the dump, Dad had to come with us and show identification proving his residency in the city. With the three of us snug in the front seat driving through the snow, we proceeded to fill the dump with years of accumulation.

By the end of the week, we had cleaned out all but my Dad's tools and some things in the cellar. I left this task for my brother to tackle.

The next day it only took the movers a few hours to efficiently carry out the furniture and boxes marked for Savannah. The house that took fifty-eight and a half years to fill was now empty.

We spent the night in the empty house, Mom and Dad sleeping on their old mattress and Jim and I on an air mattress.

GOING HOME (4/4/2008)

The next day on Jim's and my tenth anniversary, Mom and Dad posed for a last picture on their front porch and said goodbye to their old home.

I sensed some remorse, but neither parent shed a tear. It took all the energy I had not to break down and cry. I was saying farewell to a big part of my life, too. It was not just a house, but a home filled with love and good memories.

My parents were a little apprehensive on the drive to Savannah, but I also sensed a great deal of relief.

They spent the next two weeks with us while their apartment at the retirement residence was getting cleaned and painted.

I kept thanking God for the miracle of getting them to move.

CHAPTER 2
THE
ADJUSTMENT

OUR NEW HOME (4/12/2008)

Today, Mom and Dad moved into their new apartment in Savannah Seniors. The only way to describe their transition was miraculous, but my euphoria did not last long.

Because my parents grew up during the Depression, they always "saved for their old age."

Unlike my friends' mothers, mine would set and color her own hair, and never had a problem wearing the same dress to several events. I remembered asking her why she didn't want a new dress for an occasion.

"Who is going to look at me? If all they have to think about is my dress, then that's their problem," she responded.

Saving for their children's education and their old age was more important than any new dress.

Dad had his own way of saving money. He paid cash for every car he owned and ran it until it was ready for the grave.

They never wanted to be a burden on anyone and lived a comfortable but never extravagant life. Dad was a hard-working provider and Mary a conscientious saver. Through both their efforts and

Dad's pensions, they were able to afford living in a retirement community. I figured out all their expenses, and it was actually cheaper than keeping up their home.

They both loved the idea of living closer to me and Jim.

I believed making their new living arrangements feel like home was most important. We had as much of their furniture as possible moved, and arranged the bedroom and living room the same way they were in their old home, with one exception. Dad wanted a queen-size bed. After sleeping with the same woman for almost fifty-nine years in a double bed, Dad wanted a larger one. I asked him why.

With a slight grin he replied, "Well, your mother snores, and this way we are farther away from each other. But don't tell her you know she snores."

Jim and I were amazed at how quickly they adapted to the routine and activities in their new environment. Surprisingly, they rarely mentioned the old home. That baffled me, but I believed the security of living close to me outweighed the loss of their home.

Every Thursday morning Dad would go to Men's Club. The club offered two of Dad's favorite activities – watching movies and eating donuts.

Mom never missed her twice-a-week Bingo, and she loved her glass of wine during Monday night happy hour. They even went to chair aerobics three times a week. Both of them agreed: it was the best decision they had ever made.

Mom was quick to tell everyone what she loved the most. "I don't have to shop for groceries; I don't have to cook them; and the best part is I don't have to clean up after dinner."

I overheard her tell family and friends, "If you have to live in a place like this, this one is very nice, and the people are friendly."

ICE CREAM (5/8/2008)

I tried to get Mom and Dad out at least once a week and purposely made it a different day and time each week. I found varying the activity, the day, and the time, worked well and avoided a routine. I observed that a change in routine caused confusion and disappointment.

One of Mom's favorite outings was a drive for ice cream. The first time Jim and I took them; I glanced down and saw an eighty-four-year-old child. Mom grinned like a child and stated, "I want vanilla, and can I have those on top?" She was pointing to the M&M's. "Wow, look! They have nuts too. Can I have those too, please, please?"

I replied as a mother would, "Mom it's lunchtime. How about eating a sandwich first, and then having the ice cream?"

She was quick to answer. "I'm not a child, I'm not hungry, and I know what I want."

As parents know, you choose your battles wisely, and this was one I was going to lose. "Okay, Mom." As I handed her the ice cream, the happiness in her face melted my heart.

At that point, I realized my life was changing. My parents and I had switched roles, and there was no turning back. A turning point had been reached in all of our lives. I wondered if I was prepared to handle my new role.

GRAY HAIR (6/14/2008)

I never colored my hair and accepted the color Mother Nature planned for me to have, but my Mom had been coloring hers for years. Her chestnut brown hair got lighter and lighter until it was what I lovingly referred to it as "old-age blond." After almost sixty years of dying her hair, she shocked us when she announced that she no longer wanted to have her hair colored.

Asked why, she answered simply. "All the southern ladies are gray, and I'm tired of wasting my time getting my hair colored. I have better things to do."

For the first time in my life I saw my mother with gray hair. It was beautiful, and her natural wave came back. She didn't look older, just prettier.

Dad was also excited with the new look. "I feel like I'm with a new woman," he proclaimed.

I believed mom did this to fit into her new environment. In Connecticut, all her friends still colored their hair, but in her new community the color of choice was gray.

THE WATCH (7/10/2008)

While driving Mom and Dad home after dinner at our house, Dad mentioned his watch no longer lit up. He sounded so disappointed. I asked him if I could take a look to see what was wrong.

"There's nothing you can do", he immediately responded. "It's broken."

But reluctantly took off the watch and handed it to me. I pushed the stem in, and the light turned on.

He was pleased. "Gee, that's great. I wonder what I was doing wrong. Maybe I kept trying during the day and couldn't see the light."

WHAT TO DO? (7/13/2008)

Upon moving to Savannah my parents readily handed over their finances to me or, truth be known, I simply took over. I was afraid that Mom who had handled the finances would make a costly mistake. It was taking her hours to pay a few bills. She would start writing a check and the next minute had forgotten what she was doing. I soon determined that neither one had a clue as to how much money they had invested and where.

Taking the advice of friends who had elderly parents, I tackled the job of getting my Mom and Dad's finances organized.

After sorting through boxes of paperwork and excellent notes written by my father, I was able to sort out their financial status.

I was lucky because Dad had everything written down and dated; banks, bank account numbers, stocks, life insurance, and annuities. He documented everything on note paper, neatly printed in all capital letters.

I found their investments scattered all over like puzzle pieces. They had a little bit of money everywhere but not a lot anywhere.

I spent hours researching the best way to manage what was left of their lifelong savings.

With the financials in place, the next tasks were powers of attorney and wills.

Jim and I brought Mom and Dad to the attorney's office to answer some questions and sign the required paperwork. The power of attorney went smoothly, but the living will was another story.

The attorney started with Dad. When asked whether he wished to be buried or cremated, Dad quickly replied, "Cremated." Then he looked at me and asked, "Isn't that what you're going to do?"

I replied, "Yes, but you should do what *you* want."

He hesitated for only a second and replied again, "Cremated."

Then the attorney turned to Mom and asked the same question. Her smile turned to a troubled frown, and she did not reply.

He asked again. This time she turned to my father and asked what his answer was.

"Cremated," he replied.

Still she did not answer. Everyone in the room looked uncomfortable, so I asked Mom if she understood the question.

"Of course I do. I'm afraid if I say cremation, the burning will hurt."

Laughing, I answered, "Mom, you'll be dead and won't feel a thing."

"Okay, then I will be cremated too."

As we walked out to the car, Mom turned to Dad and said, "Isn't it nice to have a chief administrative assistant that handles your affairs."

Then she turned toward me, "You're adding up points to heaven."

WALMART (8/1/2008)

At least once a month and always when their apartment bill arrived Mom and I had the same conversation.

"Are we running out of money?" She asked.

I reassured her that they had enough to live on.

"What will we do when it runs out?" She questioned.

I smiled and gave her a hug. "I'll have to send both of you back to work."

Mom knew I was teasing, but after a long pause her answer was simple:

"We can be Walmart greeters. 'Welcome to Walmart,'" she shouted in her most cheerful voice.

Jim bought Mom a Walmart baseball cap he found at our church thrift store. Now she was ready to go to work, if necessary.

EVERYTHING IS BROKEN (8/14/2008)

Over the previous year, Dad reported that several things no longer worked.

The coffee pot overflowed. That was true if you filled the water reservoir twice, thinking you can make more coffee, but not understanding that the pot doesn't hold two potfuls of water.

The electric razor stopped working. It had to be recharged by plugging it in.

The lamps wouldn't turn on. Only if not switched on from the light switch on the wall, or when burnt-out light bulbs were not replaced.

The clock stopped running. If you didn't replace the batteries.

The TV remote control did not work. This occurred when the batteries were taken out and never replaced.

This was sad. There was a time when Dad could fix anything. His inability to handle simple daily-living tasks concerned me. At this point, I knew I had made the right decision to move them closer to me. They needed my help.

OBEDIENCE (9/21/2008)

"I'm so glad we obeyed you and moved to Savannah."

It touched me to hear the happiness in my Mom's voice as she said these words. At the same time, it was uncomfortable to think about how the roles had changed and that my parents now felt they needed to *obey* me.

When Mom got frustrated with her inability to make her own decisions, she would call me the "the boss lady." I knew she loved me, but she hated the fact that I was telling them what to do. Little did she know, I also hated having to tell them what to do.

I tried to make light of this title by telling her, "The title is impressive, but the pay is next to nothing." These words brought a smile to her face.

FEET (10/7/2008)

I was not sure why but I happened to look down at my mother's feet and noticed her toenails hanging out over her sandals. They were a disaster. I asked her how often she cut her toenails, and she could not remember.

"It's hard to get down there when you reach our age."

I went to get the nail clipper, sat on the floor, and proceeded to cut Mom's toenails. I could not begin to describe the effort. Her nails were not only long but thick, more like spikes than nails. Several times I thought the nail clipper would break. I was also cutting through layers of cuticle. She sat there smiling and so happy that she was getting a pedicure. After twenty minutes, I gave up but felt they were a hundred percent better and quickly applied some polish to cover them up. She kept repeating how lucky she was to have such a good daughter. All I kept repeating in my mind was, *"Ugh."*

As I moved across the floor to Dad's chair, I was asking myself why I was doing this. In the Bible, the washing of the feet was an act of love and humility. At the time I felt neither. I removed his socks and immediately put them back on and suggested we go to a podiatrist.

The visit to the podiatrist later in the week went well except it consumed a great deal of time. The total trip took me over two hours from the time I left my house, picked them up, drove to the podiatrist's office, sat through two appointments and then drove them home. Now that their nails were more manageable, if I cut them myself, it could be accomplished during a visit and would take less than thirty minutes.

Maybe I was looking for humility because I had to love my parents to do this. Old feet are ugly.

A few months later, a bright idea came to me. I purchased rubber gloves and two dishpans, black and red, and headed over to my parents' apartment.

I filled the pans with antibacterial soap, alcohol, which is supposed to kill everything, and water. Then I had them soak their feet for ten minutes before I put on my rubber gloves and tackled the job. The effort was easier, and the job was completed in fifteen minutes. I must admit their feet looked a lot better, and I saved hours. But I still didn't feel the humility.

CLEAN CLOTHES (11/11/2008)

From the first day Mom moved into her apartment, she had been good about doing the laundry. Laundering their sheets and towels was one of the services included in their rent, but residents were responsible for washing their personal clothing.

Mom never had a clothes dryer, and up until the day they moved to Savannah, she dried their clothes on the clothesline.

I would always remember her carrying in our jeans from the clothesline in the winter. They were frozen solid and stood up as if someone was inside them.

Now Mom insisted she must wash clothes at least three times a week. I concluded meeting in the laundry room was a social event. The only problem was that everything went into the dryer. Several of Dad's sweaters shrunk to toddler size, but at least they had clean clothes.

STORIES (12/25/2008)

Holidays in our household were proceeded by days of cooking. Church and family dinner was the main focus of any holiday. My family spent hours eating, telling stories, laughing, and then, complaining that we ate too much.

Mom had her favorite stories and loved to share them with everyone. Her storytelling became a tradition.

This Christmas in Savannah had been no different. Mom started out by asking Jim and our son-in-law, Ricardo, if they ever heard a particular story. They would look at each other, smile, and in unison say. "No, we never heard that story."

Now the stories were not narrated a few times a year but repeated several times during the same dinner. Mom would forget and tell the story many times.

"Have you heard this story?" She would ask again.

This time Jim and Ricardo not just smiled but laughed and once again said, "No, we never heard that story."

Mom was smart enough to recognize that the laughter meant she had already told the story.

She laughed and said, "I don't care if you already heard it. I like this story and I'm going to tell it again."

Mom's memory was leaving her, bit by bit every day, but her sense of humor and quick wit remained as sharp as ever. She was still able to perform the tasks required for daily living independently. I hoped and prayed the year to come would not change that.

CHAPTER 3
YEAR TWO

HELPING LEONARD (1/12/2009)

Mom and Dad had been devoted to one another for almost sixty years. Mom had always taken care of Dad, or at least the family always thought she did.

During one of Jim and my visits, she asked Dad if he was okay. Then she came out with the following response, we were both shocked and broke into laughter.

"Len, are you okay? Is something bothering you? Well, if there is, take it to Jesus. I can't help you anymore, but He probably can."

FALLING (3/22/2009)

I had worried about one of my parents falling. It might be because my grandfather fell in his eighties and died shortly thereafter. Or maybe I was recalling stories heard from friends about their experiences with parents. It was a fact that falling was the leading cause of injury death among people sixty-five and older.

A good friend of mine from Connecticut called to tell me about her mother falling. Dotty, at eighty-six, decided one day in the cold of winter to bring inside her potted winter-killed geranium plant to water. Dotty still lived at home with her husband, Fred, and was in the early stages of Alzheimer's. As she carried the large ceramic pot into the kitchen, she slipped on the kitchen rug. Both Dotty and the pot went flying. Dotty landed right on the kitchen floor, and the pot went through a kitchen cabinet before stopping.

She immediately called out to her husband to help her up. Fred, suffering from Parkinson's disease, was not the most stable individual. As Dotty tried to lift herself using Fred's pant leg, she pushed him off balance, and down he came.

Now Dotty, Fred, and the potted geranium are all on the kitchen floor. Rather than bother one of their four children, they decided to crawl to the phone and call their next door neighbor Charley. This sounded like a good solution to me until my friend explained. "Charley only has one leg."

I laughed every time I recalled this story.

Charley called his son to help. Dotty and Fred got up without any major injuries.

I envisioned this being my parents, and knew their choice would have been the same. They would rather exhaust all possible options before calling my brother or me for help.

I decided no matter how old parents were, they shared the belief that their children were suppose to rely on them, and they should not rely on their children.

COUNT ON IT (3/29/2009)

Issues with my parents inevitably occurred when we were out of town. Jim and I went to Asheville, North Carolina, with friends for a few days. Sunday morning at eleven, my cell phone rang. My daughter's phone number appeared on the screen. Marisa lived a two-and-a-half-hour drive from Savannah. She called her grandparents often, and I anticipated her call was to notify me Mom and Dad were okay. Well, not quite.

"Mom, Grandpa fell getting out of bed, and can't get up. Grandma said he's fine. I told her I was going to call the front desk for help and she got angry with me. She said she would call."

For a moment my heart stopped. I thanked Marisa for letting me know, and I immediately hung up. I called my parents.

"Mom, where's Pop?" I asked

"He is in the bedroom," she told me.

"Is he okay?"

"Well, he's okay but on the floor. He can't get up."

"How long has he been on the floor?"

"I don't know."

"Have you called anyone for help?"

"Not yet, but I will."

"Mom, please call the front desk for help, and I'll call you back."

Residents received a daily call from the security guard checking to see if they were alright. I never found out why Mom did not report Dad's fall to the security guard. I was not sure how long he had been on the floor or would have remained on the floor if Marisa hadn't called me.

I knew one thing, similar to Dotty and Fred, my parents didn't like to "put anyone out."

We were a six-hour drive from Savannah. Our friends offered to drive us home, but they had scheduled to spend the day with their granddaughter. We didn't want to upset their plans unless necessary. Marisa offered to drive to Savannah, but Jim advised I call someone to check on Dad before making any decisions.

That afternoon I made a dozen calls to friends whose help made me understand that good friends were a gift. They checked on Dad, brought him a walker, and even helped arrange a full-time caregiver to stay with my parents until we arrived home. Dad was not in pain, just tired.

We cut our trip short, and returned the next day. I called the doctor as soon as we got to Mom and Dad's apartment. The doctor suggested we wait until morning to take Dad to the emergency room. I spent the night with Mom and Dad.

Dad's walking was unstable and slow. I helped him get to bed, and hoped he would sleep through the night. It never occurred to me that he would need my help going to the bathroom.

A friend whose father was in a nursing home said I hadn't experienced anything until I saw my father naked.

Another friend revealed that her ninety-year-old mother asked her to wipe her ass after a bowel movement. She was still in shock when her mother added, "I wiped your ass when you were young, and so you should be able to wipe mine."

Hearing both friends share their stories, I knew my parents would never put me in that type of position. They were too proud and modest. Brother was I wrong.

Poor Dad needed help getting in and out of bed and into the bathroom all night. He got up every half hour to urinate. Mom was by his side every time and tried her best to get him out of bed, but without my help they would have both ended up on the floor.

So as any good daughter would, I tried to look the other way as I pulled down his undershorts. I was not going to view my father's private parts. I realized at this point my Dad no longer had any shame or embarrassment. He could care less that I saw his old, shriveled parts. All he wanted was help. None of us got any sleep, and I could now say that I had experienced it all.

NORMAL PRESSURE HYDROCEPHALUS (3/24/2009)

The next morning, I rode in the ambulance that took Dad to the emergency room. Jim and Mom followed behind in our car.

After days of testing, Dad was seen by two neurologists. The first doctor said she was uncertain as to the problem but thought it might be Parkinson's disease. I found that hard to believe, since Dad never had any type of shaking. She informed me that her partner, who was more skilled in geriatrics, would be in to see Dad the next day.

The following afternoon the second doctor spent about ten minutes with Dad. The doctor's quick examination surprised me. I caught up with him at the nurses' station updating Dad's chart. He asked me if I had access to the Internet. When I replied positively he said.

"Normal pressure hydrocephalus. Look it up and let me know if the symptoms describe your father. If so, I can arrange for a surgeon to operate next week."

Hearing the word *operate* worried me. I had heard of hydrocephalus in babies but never adults. I left the hospital perplexed.

As soon as I got home, I went straight for the computer. My search listed hundreds of sites with information.

Normal pressure hydrocephalus (NPH) was a condition that occurred when an abnormal amount of cerebrospinal fluid (CSF) accumulated in the ventricles of the brain. I learned the causes of the condition were unclear, but the symptoms described Dad perfectly. The symptoms were very subtle and worsen very gradually which is why the condition might be attributed to old age.

Jim and I noticed Dad's walking had become more like a shuffle and he was often hesitant in taking the first step. He would walk for a short period and then stop as if he were frozen trying to figure out what to do next. When spoken to, he often acted confused and turned to Mom for the answers. Dad seemed to be having problems communicating. I wrote his difficulties off to old age.

The urinary incontinence was another symptom of NPH, and had begun after Dad's fall. I could not believe what I was reading. I suddenly realized his issues were not a result of old age. Something could be done to enhance his quality of life.

Before deciding to operate, the doctor performed a lumbar puncture to remove some of the excess fluid, and observed Dad for thirty to sixty minutes to determine if the symptoms improved. The procedure, although temporary, made a remarkable difference, especially in Dad's cognitive ability. He was talking again, asking questions and joking. After witnessing my Dad after the test, I signed the approval for the operation.

He was operated on the following week. The neurosurgeon surgically implanted a shunt in Dad's head behind his right ear to drain the fluid from the brain. When the fluid builds up, the one-way shunt opened and drained the excess fluid into the abdomen, where it gets absorbed. The operation was successful, thanks to the skilled neurosurgeon, abdominal surgeon, and the wonderful hospital staff.

His recovery was amazing. In total, he spent four weeks in the hospital, of which two were for rehabilitation. Mom and I went to see him every day. She would spend most of the day by his side. Her devotion could be described only as true love.

The operation seemed to cause one problem. For as long as I could recall, Dad had an unbelievable appetite. He could easily out eat anyone I knew and was generally not picky. So when he refused to eat the hospital food, I worried. The nurses would try to find out what he wanted, and he only asked for hamburgers and grilled cheese sandwiches - very childlike indeed. He also loved to drink Ensure. To him, they were milkshakes. Thanks to Chick-fil-A, Krispy Kreme, and Wendy's, Dad was getting his nutrition. Without his chicken sandwiches, donuts and Frostys, he would never have survived.

I joked with Jim that maybe his new dietary preferences were a result of draining too much fluid from his brain.

DOUBLE-D's (3/25/2009)

Mom stayed with us while Dad was in the hospital. Every night, I made sure she took her pills, and tucked her into bed. Yes, tucked her in bed. She was lost without Dad and that made her feel better. It also made me feel better knowing she was in bed and not up wandering around. She put a picture of Dad on the empty pillow next to her.

One night I knocked on the door and asked if I could come in. "Sure," she replied.

Walking into the room I was greeted by my mother naked from the waist up. I saw more then I could ever have imagined.

My Mom was all of four feet ten inches tall. From the waist down she wore a size twelve, but from the waist up, she made Dolly Parton look small. Her 44 double-D's were on display.

With a tone of disgust I commanded, "Cover up. You are displaying more than I want to see."

"Haven't you seen boobs before? You're acting like it's the first time."

THAT DEPENDS (4/1/2009)

After his fall at home, Dad's bladder control was close to zero. The doctors all agreed it would improve in time after the operation. With a slumping posture, Dad stood about five feet two inches tall and weighed 160 pounds.

While visiting him one afternoon in the hospital, the physical therapist came by for his daily therapy session. I decided to walk with them and stayed a good distance behind, so I wouldn't be in the way.

I can still visualize my short, slightly bent-over Dad strolling down the hall pushing his walker. As he proceeded, I noticed his stride was getting longer. I soon understood why as his one-size-fits-all adult diaper was gradually falling lower and lower until it hit the floor. I couldn't help but chuckle.

The physical therapist reached down and picked up the diaper, and continued walking. The diaper was so huge it could have protected all three of us. It was even funnier to see this young woman walking with one hand on the belt strapped around my Dad's waist and her other hand holding up the diaper.

At that point I decided to buy correct-fitting diapers. I was not sure if there was any significance in the fact I was doing this on April Fools' Day.

I soon realized a good-fitting diaper did not exist. I was amazed at both the variety and sizing of such a necessity. Men's protective underwear products came in pads, tape-ons and pull-ups. The only consistent fact was they were all white.

I understood the difference between regular and extra absorbent. I assumed one worked better at night than during the day, but how was I supposed to know how much urine my father passed? The other confusing part was the sizing. Small-medium ran from waist sizes 34-44. My Dad wore size 38 pants. I figured small-medium would be a good fit.

When I got to the cashier, I asked for them to be double bagged. I didn't want my Dad to be embarrassed, but later I realized that at his age, one no longer got embarrassed. I guessed it was me who was embarrassed.

ARICEPT (4/22/2009)

After spending four weeks in the hospital, Dad was more than ready to get home. Mom was thrilled to be going back to her apartment with Dad.

Exiting the hospital, the usual follow-up appointments and prescriptions were handed to me. Numbness came over me as I quickly glanced at the list of medications. Oh, no, not him too.

The doctor had never mentioned an issue with my father's memory. I believed the Aricept had helped delay the progression of memory loss in my mother and hoped that it would do the same for Dad.

PILLS (4/23/2009)

When Dad returned home from the hospital, I decided a nightly pill reminder call would be helpful until they got back into a routine.

"Hi Mom, I called to remind you and Pop to take your pills."

"We make you old, don't we? What day is today?" She asked.

"It's Tuesday. Now please get up and take your pills." I knew she was sitting down watching TV as she did every night. If I hung up, the pills would never be taken.

Their pills were stored by day in pillboxes with their names clearly written on them.

"Do I have to do it now? I'm good at this stuff. I'm not getting up, but I'll remember later."

"Please do it now," I pleaded.

"Okay. Today is Monday, right?"

"No, it's Tuesday."

"Now what do you want me to do?"

"Take your pills."

"Hold on. Is today Monday?"

"It's Tuesday."

"Okay, all these pills must get mixed up and melt together in the belly. How does God know what He's doing in there? You are the best daughter. Thank you. I was of some importance before, you know. You had to have me before you could be born."

"You are still important to me," I said with a heavy heart.

I knew there were days that some of the pills were forgotten, and I wondered how many nights she had taken his pills and he, hers. At least two of the pills they both take at night were the same.

PHYSICAL THERAPHY (4/27/2009)

Dad had two weeks of physical therapy in the hospital and needed two more weeks upon discharge. Their independent-living community provided therapy services, which made it very convenient. I decided to be there for his first session.

The physical therapist came to the apartment to pick Dad up. I was there when she appeared at the door. After Dad signed some paperwork, she escorted him out into the hall. Mom grabbed her cane and followed right behind.

The therapist appeared puzzled, but Mom smiled and explained. "We're a package deal. I go where he goes, and he goes where I go."

After the third session, I received a call from the physical therapist. I knew this could not be good news. She proceeded to inform me that she had a concern. I asked her if Dad was not doing well.

"Oh no, your Dad is doing great," she replied. "I'm worried about your mother. She is very unstable on her feet and tires easily. She's the one who needs a walker."

Believe it or not, I was pleased to hear this. I had been trying to get my Mom to use a walker for months. Now I could blame someone else for the "four-wheel vehicle."

RED & BLUE WALKERS (4/28/2009)

Jim and I picked Mom and Dad up for lunch, and I felt it would be a good time to address the subject of walkers. I had contacted their doctor and he agreed with the physical therapist: it was time for walkers.

"We bought you a surprise."

"Oh, really? How nice. What did you buy me?" She asked, enthusiastically.

"We got you a rolling walker."

"What! Those are for old people."

"How old do you have to be to have a walker?" I asked her.

"Well, I have five years to go. I'm not old until I reach ninety. I don't want a walker. Why did you get that for me?"

"Your doctor said you needed one and so did Pop's physical therapist."

"How do they know me? I've never been to a doctor here."

Mom had seen the doctor every three months for a year now and saw the physical therapist the day before.

"Oh, look, a blue car and a yellow car. Why do I need this walker?"

"Mom, everyone says it will help you."

"Who is this 'everyone' you are talking to, and how do they know you?"

"Everyone knows me, Mom."

"I know, and that's because I tell them you are my daughter. Oh, look, a yellow car."

"Mom, didn't you promise me earlier that you would at least try using the walker?"

"Do you have that in writing?"

After lunch, we went back to their apartment and assembled the walkers. Mom would not even look at hers.

One week later during my routine morning call, Mom informed me, "I have a walker. It's shiny red, and I love it."

Go figure!

THE SHOWER (5/1/2009)

When Dad got home from the hospital, I had arranged to have someone help him shower every other day. This was an extra-charge service the facility provided. I bought a shower chair to make the task easier.

After a couple of weeks, I decided to ask if the arrangement was working out. Dad's reply was simple. With a grin one usually sees on a mischievous child, he answered, "It's working out fine but I get to wash my essential parts."

My mother had also begun to have issues bathing; I believed she developed a fear of falling in the shower. She now gave herself a sponge bath every day. She refused to use the shower chair and insisted upon washing as she put it "the old way."

Today I asked her if she needs someone to help her shower.

"Oh, yeah, and make sure he's a big hunk," she answered.

At least she was washing herself, and I guess there was nothing wrong with the old sponge bath.

BIRTHDAY SURPRISE (5/3/2009)

Today my mother informed me Dad had blood in his urine. Dad has had prostate cancer for more than ten years. When I questioned her if he was in pain, she answered, "Talk to him."

"Dad, how are you feeling?"

"I feel fine."

"Are you in pain?"

"No."

"Did you have blood in your urine?"

"Only a little."

I hung up, and tried to figure out what to do next. Today was my birthday, and selfishly I did not want to spend it in the emergency room.

"Let's bring Mom and Dad here for breakfast and assess his condition," I suggested to Jim.

Jim should have asked who made me the doctor, but I think he wanted me to have a relaxing birthday. Emergency rooms were anything but relaxing.

Dad seemed a little tired but not much different than on other days. I called his doctor and when we didn't get a response after an hour, we drove them back to their apartment so Mom would not miss her Sunday Bingo.

Sure enough, when we got home there was a message from the doctor's office advising us to go to the emergency room. So, back to get my parents and off to the hospital, we went. As we waited in the emergency room, my Dad turned to my mother and asked: "What are we doing here?"

"I don't know. Mariann, what are we doing here?" She asked.

I answered her question, and smiled at Jim.

Dad finally got admitted and led to a room. It was painted entirely in beige and measured all of eight feet by eight feet. It reminded me of a prison cell. I couldn't help thinking how the wait might have been more enjoyable if the walls were painted in bright, cheery colors.

After examining Dad, a young woman doctor explained my father needed a catheter. She tested Dad's urine for infection, and told us to see a urologist the next day. She also informed me he would likely have to go home with the catheter. At that point, I wasn't sure if I should laugh or cry. All I could imagine was the drainage bag overflowing all over the place in the middle of the night. Was this doctor serious?

I tried to picture my mother, a sleepy eighty-five-year-old with dementia, trying to help her husband empty a urine-filled drainage bag. First she would have to remember that he had one. I guessed my facial expression said it all. Somewhat sarcastically, I asked the doctor if she thought my father was capable of emptying a drainage bag. I never got an answer.

The tests determined that Dad had a urinary infection. We left the emergency room two hours later with two prescriptions and no drainage bag. I didn't understand why the doctor said Dad needed a catheter and sent him home without one.

That night I called mom to make sure Dad was taking his bladder infection pills. "Mom, has Pop taken his pills?"

"The brown pills, right? She asked. Are these for me?"

"No, they're for Pop. He has a urinary infection."

"Oh, yeah, he has a pisser problem. Maybe I'll take these pills, too. They look like chocolate. Maybe they taste like it."

YELLOW CARS (5/12/2009)

I wondered if there was a medical explanation for my mother's fixation with cars these days. Ever since she moved to Savannah, she has been fascinated with yellow cars in particular. The conversation was always the same and happened every time she was in our car.

"Look, Jim, a yellow car. I've never seen a yellow car. Jim, would you buy a yellow car?"

"Yes, I would buy a yellow car," he would reply.

"I would never buy a yellow car. I like blue cars."

After a year, Mom continued with her fixation with yellow cars. Each time she started with the yellow-car routine, my husband and I lovingly looked at each other, and with a straight face Jim replied. "Yes, I would buy a yellow car."

THE LITTLE CUP (6/9/2009)

Dad had a follow-up urology appointment. After weeks of dragging both of them to the doctor's office, I thought it would be better for Mom to stay home and play Bingo. I would take Dad alone.

Upon arriving, I filled out the appropriate insurance and personal information, and then the receptionist handed me one of the infamous plastic cups. Oh my God, Dad needed to give them a sample and would need help.

Usually restrooms were private and inside, near the examination room, but not in this office. The restroom was in the back of the waiting room, and I soon found out it was not soundproof.

Dad and I walked together toward the restroom. I could see the smiles on those around us in the waiting room. We had to pass by at least eight people before reaching our destination. His walker wouldn't fit through the door, which was an indication of how small the restroom was. Dad walked in first and I followed.

Dad proceeded to drop his pants including his diaper. This was the first time I realized that the diapers were made without a front fly. I handed him the cup but could not avoid looking at the small, shriveled part of his anatomy that helped in my creation. I turned the water on to help him get in the mood. After what seemed like hours, I pulled up his diaper and his pants, instructed him to wash his hands, and walked out into the waiting room carrying an empty cup.

That time the smiles were wider noticing me with the empty cup.

All I could think about was that we could not leave until Dad made a deposit in the cup. We would have to go through the exercise again.

At that point, I knew that at fifty-eight years old, I was no longer the child and was now all grown up. I also learned that day helping Dad wasn't as bad the second time. On the second try, Dad was able to fill a small portion of the cup.

Two weeks later, we returned to the urologist for another check-up. This time I brought my mother along. I felt it was her responsibility to accompany her husband into the tiny bathroom, not mine.

I had prepared her during the car trip that she needed to go into the restroom and help her husband.

When we arrived, Mom and Dad sat down, and I went to sign him in and get the cup.

The waiting room was even busier than during our first visit. I led Dad in the direction of the bathroom. Mom was not moving. In a whisper I reminded her that she needed to help Dad get his specimen. In a loud voice she replied, "Why should I go with him? He's a big boy and knows how to pee."

After a few convincing words from me, she finally got up. By this time Dad was already trying to remove the paint on the door frame by pushing his walker through the extremely small door. Taking the walkers, I gently pushed both of them into the restroom and handed Mom the cup.

I sat in the waiting room, glanced up, and saw a room filled with smiling faces. One kind woman mouthed, *Bless you.* At that moment I could hear my mother.

"Len, can't you pee a little more? There's not enough in this cup. We don't have all day."

Now the smiles became laughs.

As she instructed him to wash his hands, I knocked on the door, took the cup, and started to lead them out. Mom immediately said, "Wait! With all this talk of peeing, now I have to go."

This trip to the urologist was not much better than the previous visit.

THE STOLEN (6/11/2009)

For about a year now, Mom had been reporting missing items. It started with perfume and worked its way to shampoo. The item was different, but the conversation started the same.

"Hi, Mom. How are you and Pop today?"

In her most serious voice she answers, "We're good, but I have to tell you they stole my perfume."

"Not sure why anyone wants your perfume, but I'll help you look for it the next time I come see you."

"No sense of you looking. I've already searched all over the place and didn't find it. I know you don't believe me, but they do steal. They would take the gold out of my teeth if I had any."

"Who would take your perfume?"

"I don't know, just they would."

The first thing "they" had stolen was a bottle of her favorite perfume, Estee Lauder Pleasures. There was an empty bottle on her dresser, and I can't refute her claim since I don't remember if she had a new bottle or not. The perfume was never found.

The next missing item was a gold-and-diamond man's ring. This was more serious. My mother had started wearing the ring recently. Her arthritic fingers restricted wearing other rings except her wedding band. The ring was made by my grandfather, Dad's father, who was a jeweler.

Jim and I went to their apartment immediately and started the search.

Growing up Catholic made me a believer in praying to St. Anthony to assist me in recovering lost items. Through the years he and I had developed a real friendship. My husband found this amusing, but St. Anthony and I had recovered many of Mom's lost items.

During the third search in the sofa, I happened to glance at the table next to the sofa. There on the second shelf was the ring.

The diamond ring was followed by the missing deodorant.

"Now they took my new stick of deodorant."

"Mom, who would want to take someone else's deodorant?"

"Well, someone that smells bad."

The deodorant was also found.

On another occasion while driving Dad to the doctor's office, she notified Jim and I their shampoo was missing.

"Do you know they took the shampoo?"

"Shampoo?" I repeated.

"Yes, and I searched all over for it."

"Mom, it's got to be somewhere. Who wants shampoo?"

"Maybe someone took it because they needed it more than we do."

"Maybe, but I doubt it. I'll look for it when we take you home."

"No need. Where are you going to look that I haven't already looked? The refrigerator?"

"Mom, how do you come up with these answers?"

"I don't know. Things come into my head but unfortunately they don't stay in there very long," she replied with a laugh.

The first place I looked when we got to their apartment was the shower. Lo and behold, the shampoo sat right where it was supposed to be, on the shelf in their shower.

Friends shared similar stories about their parents and misplaced items.

It was totally unlike my mother to accuse anyone of stealing, let alone imply that a staff member would take something from her. This was strange behavior. Maybe she felt better presuming it was someone else and not her lapse of memory.

NO REGRETS (6/4/2009)

I stopped by to visit my parents today. Having forgotten their apartment key at home, I knocked on their door. No answer. I turned the doorknob, jiggling the dead bolt. No answer. I called out, "Pop, Mom". No answer. I repeated this three times and then decided they must have taken a walk.

I went down to the end of the hallway and saw the familiar red walker. Mom was sitting at the puzzle table at the end of the hallway, working away. She immediately stopped to greet me. Mom loved to make puzzles, and I was happy to see her doing something she enjoyed.

She added a few more pieces to the puzzle then we walked back to her apartment. She was excited to tell me that they had gone to the ice-cream social that day, and it was wonderful.

"I had a double scoop."

"Two scoops? Mom, that's not good for your weight."

"If I didn't have the second scoop and died today, I'd have regrets all the way to heaven. I don't want to die with regrets."

I smiled and it occurred to me that she was still giving me good advice.

Dad was sound asleep in the apartment no more than eight feet from the front door. He never heard my knocking and calling out.

PAPER PRODUCTS (6/10/2009)

I think growing up during the Great Depression instilled a fear in my Dad of running out of paper products. Whenever we went to a restaurant, he stuffed extra paper napkins into his pockets.

Several months before being diagnosed with normal pressure hydrocephalus, Dad surprised Jim and me during a visit. As Jim and I walked into their building, we noticed Dad moving toward the elevators. He was wearing a sweater, as he usually does, but it bulged on one side. When we got into his apartment, I questioned the bulge. He looked puzzled and lifted the sweater. There was a roll of toilet paper hidden under his sweater. He must have taken it from the lobby restroom.

I could understand and justify the need if their front hall closet didn't already have at least fifteen rolls of toilet paper.

Restroom paper towels and Kleenex were also an attraction to Dad. One day, I asked if he needed anything from the store, and without hesitation, he answered, "Kleenex."

I decided to check the closet first. Carrying six unopened boxes over to him, I asked how many more he needed. We both laughed.

I think my parents were environmentalists well before it had become popular. They would use a sheet of paper towel and then hung it over the roll to dry and reused it.

ONE MORE TIME (6/21/2009)

After a recent visit to the urologist, the doctor recommended Dad undergo a *cystoscopy*, a procedure that allowed the doctor to look inside the urethra and bladder. The procedure was done using a cystoscope which is a telescope like instrument. The cystoscope was inserted, and a sterile fluid is put into the bladder to expand it. The procedure was performed in the doctor's office. Even though it sounded painful, the doctor assured me it wasn't.

Years ago, Dad had prostate issues and some tumors were found in his bladder. The doctor believed it would be wise to check his bladder.

As I get older, I get wiser. My Mom came with us again this time, to help Dad with his specimen sample. I found a private restroom inside the office. Dad was successful, and I was happy thinking the visit was going to be a piece of cake.

I left Mom in the waiting room and walked Dad into the procedure room. I helped him get undressed and put on his hospital gown. The nurse instructed him to sit on what looked like the most uncomfortable chair I'd seen. He seemed to be exhausted.

I decided to leave the room to check on Mom. Upon returning to Dad's room, the nurse suggested I wait there with him. I sat down in a chair opposite him, and as I glanced up, all I could see was a clear view of my Dad's crown jewels. I've never jumped up so fast in my life. At that moment the doctor came in. He asked if I wanted to sit down, and stay during the procedure. I muttered that I had seen enough for one day and quickly left the room.

Less than fifteen minutes later the doctor walked briskly to the nurse's station, and asked if he had a target on his back. I immediately knew what had happened. My Dad had hit the target and had managed to wet the doctor's pant leg all the way down to his shoes. Ironically, I thought, now he goes without a problem.

Embarrassed, I apologized to the doctor. He was great and said it happened to him all the time. With a grin I replied, "Maybe you should consider another career."

I went into the room to help Dad get dressed. He had no idea that he had just given the doctor a shower.

RABBIT (7/1/2009)

The month after Dad retired at sixty-five years old, he started a tradition. He had heard somewhere if the first word you hear on the first day of the month was *rabbit* you would have good luck all month.

For twenty-three years, he had religiously called my husband, daughter, brother, sister-in-law, nephew, and me to wish us "rabbit" early in the morning the first day of every month. He would call me at eight in the morning. No matter what I was doing, I would excuse myself and pick up the phone to hear his familiar voice say, "rabbit."

Today, Dad did not call. I could not describe my disappointment. Jim asked several times if Dad had called. Both my daughter and brother called me to see if everything was all right.

Dad had forgotten to call after all these years. No one wanted to call Dad and make him feel bad about forgetting. It was a sad day.

I was having difficulty accepting the fact that the tradition was ending after twenty-three years. I felt part of my Dad was fading way.

HAPPY FOURTH OF JULY (7/4/2009)

I called Mom and Dad less than an hour after they returned from their noon July fourth luncheon. I asked Mom what they ate.

"I'm sure hot dogs, and I don't remember what else. We forgot what we had, but we had it, so it must have been good."

The next day I asked her what she had for dinner.

"I don't remember what we ate, but we ate it, so I'm sure we liked it because we ate it.

I thought she was becoming another Yogi Berra. He was a former Major League Baseball catcher when I was growing up, and well known for his witticisms. The witticisms often took the form of a needlessly repetitive statement.

BREAKFAST, LUNCH, AND DINNER INCLUDED (7/15/2009)

My parents' retirement facility previously provided dinner with a slight charge for lunch. Today they changed their policy to provide breakfast, lunch, and dinner free of charge to the independent-living residents.

Prior to this new policy, getting my parents up before ten in the morning was difficult. Mom and Dad no longer had an issue with getting up early and were ready before nine. They wanted to have their free breakfast.

I discussed overeating with my parents. Dad's weight had not changed since they moved. He did a good job watching what he ate. His weight was normal for his height and age. Mom on the other hand had mastered the art of changing the subject anytime her weight was mentioned. The woman who made me always eat healthily now chose anything sweet over healthy options. I blamed her new attitude partially on her medication and partially on her memory. Her weight did not bother her, and she would forget what and how much she had consumed. In the past year Mom gained fifteen pounds.

During her last visit to the doctor, he counseled her to watch the weight, but was not overly concerned. Jim believed this was a futile exercise, and at their age they should be able to eat whatever they wanted. I was concerned about their health and thinking in practical terms. I was the one who had to shop for their clothes. Mom had increased two sizes in everything except her shoes.

During a discussion with Mom, encouraging her to watch what she eats and try to eliminate white foods, she said, "If I eat too much, I'll probably get a heart attack and die. I'm going to be cremated right?"

"Right, that's what you have in your living will."

She looked pensive and came back with, "Well, I hate the heat so maybe I'll try to stay healthy. I think I'm afraid to burn."

Two months had passed since our weight discussion, and I was driving my parents to the doctor's office for their six-month checkup. Mom was very apprehensive today.

During the last checkup, she reluctantly stepped on the scale. She had gained an average of one pound for every month since she moved to Savannah. The weight gain was very noticeable. My attempts to talk to her about cutting down on the carbohydrates and fats never reached her ears. Mom loved to eat, especially anything that contained sugar and all her weight landed below her neck and above her waist. At four feet and ten inches, she was very, very top heavy.

We had a short wait before Mom got called into the examination room. As she approached the scale, she repeatedly asked if she had to be weighed. The nurse directed her toward the scale and proceeded to help her step on. I feared Mom was going to die right on the spot when she saw the scales move above the 150-pound mark.

She immediately protested. "This scale is broken! That can't be right."

After subtracting the normal two pounds for cloths, the final weight was 151 pounds. Mom blamed the weight on her overly abundant chest.

"I can't help the way I was born," she said.

I had begun to think Jim was right; worrying about my mother's weight was only stressing me out. She was happy and to me that was important.

PASTA NIGHT (7/21/2009)

Mom and Dad never complained about the food served at their facility. Dad was not a complainer. Mom was so thrilled that she didn't have to shop for food, prepare it, and clean up, any meal served was great. Jim called it "eating at a country club." The food was good, and plenty of selections were offered.

The one thing my parents did miss was homemade Italian food. We had pasta twice a week when I was growing up. In those days, it was called "macaroni," not pasta. Now, once a month, I had them over for macaroni.

I decided to make something special and prepared shells stuffed with spinach, mozzarella, and ricotta. I also made eggplant parmigiana and meatballs.

Dad was napping in front of the TV, and Mom was reading the newspaper - I'm sure for at least the third time that day.

Every half hour or so, Mom asked if I needed help, but other than that, conversation was nonexistent. Whenever I asked a question neither one could remember the answer. Eventually I stopped talking and that seemed fine with them.

I recognized at that moment whatever I did for my parents from here on out was really being done for myself. I knew they appreciated the dinner, and both commented on how delicious it was, but in an hour they would not remember what they had eaten.

I had an empty feeling in me. I felt like my parents were slowly leaving me. I guess what I was experiencing, was learning how to live without my parents. With each passing day I lost a little more of them. This is uncomfortable to write but the day they are taken away from me will be more of a celebration of their life than a sadness of their death. I'm experiencing their loss every day, little by little.

ICE CREAM (7/28/2009)

It had been over a year since our first trip out for ice cream. Now, we went for frozen yogurt instead. Mom and Dad still got excited when we took them out for a yogurt lunch. I called to ask them if they would like to come to our house for lunch or go out for yogurt.

Mom answered the phone and hesitated for a moment before replying. "Well, we really love yogurt."

I learned today that spending quality time with my parents doing what they liked was important. To them an outing for yogurt was an exciting event.

Mom would forget what day it was, what she had eaten for dinner, whom she had just spoke to on the phone, and the list went on. But she never forgot to clip the two-for-five dollar yogurt coupons from the Sunday newspaper.

THE DOLL (8/3/2009)

I am really confused about how a person's memory works. My daughter believes my mother remembers what she wants to remember.

I found my mother's baby doll while cleaning out her closet at their old house. The doll's porcelain arms and legs were off. I had the doll repaired and a new outfit made for it. I thought it would be a wonderful gift for Mom and Dad to give their great-granddaughter. The total cost for this work was thirty-five dollars. Mom insisted upon paying for the work.

Mom was impressed and pleased with the outcome. She mentioned on several occasions, "I can't wait to give Isabella the doll. Doesn't it look great? That lady who fixed it charged us only thirty-five dollars."

Why can she remember this? She struggled to remember details about her daily life, but could remember this one-time event.

The next time my granddaughter visited my parents, mom proudly gave her the doll. Isabella was too young to appreciate the doll, but the joy Mom expressed as she handed it to her great-granddaughter was priceless.

WRITE THINGS DOWN (8/6/2009)

Today Mom lamented that she can't remember things, like what she had for dinner or what they did that day. I suggested she carry a small notepad with her to write things down that she wanted to remember. She thought that was a great idea.

Four hours later I called and asked her what they had for dinner. I was checking to see if the notepad idea worked.

"I don't remember," she replied.

"Did you carry your pad with you today?'

"Well, stupid ass," she said, referring to herself, "carried the notepad downstairs and then forgot why she carried it."

My idea wasn't so great, after all.

GUILT (8/10/2009)

I explained my guilty feelings that I wasn't doing enough for my parents as a byproduct of growing up in an Italian Catholic household. Why was I now feeling guilty about my parents? They had never instilled this guilt. They constantly reassured me they were fine, and told me not to worry about them. They were very appreciative for all that I did and reminded me I had a life, too.

When they lived in Connecticut and I was too far away to be of any help, I could understand why I felt guilty. But why now? I handled their finances, drove them to the doctor, shopped, took them out at least once a week, called several times a day, and, hell, even helped with the urine samples.

After talking with friends, I realized two types of guilt exist: the caregiver's guilt and the absent child's guilt. As the caregiver, I constantly felt I should be doing more to help my parents. My brother's guilt was rooted in not being around to help me.

I decided that guilt was part of life, and maybe it had made me a more caring person.

Erma Bombeck used to say, "Guilt is the gift that never stops giving." She was right. Guilt was very generous.

SAVING A DOLLAR (8/16/2009)

Today I had lunch with Mom and Dad. They paraded me past their friends as we entered the dining room. I enjoyed making them happy, but conversation was difficult. Mom was starting to repeat herself more frequently and forgot what she had done hours before. Dad rarely spoke except when asked questions, and even then he took forever to gather his thoughts. I tried to make small-talk about the food and dining room.

After lunch, we went back to their apartment. I happened to be standing behind Mom as she opened the refrigerator to get a drink. Sitting on the bottom shelf were at least one hundred small cream containers, the kind served in restaurants with coffee.

"Mom, I think you have enough cream".

"Oh, I know. We ask for them every night at dinner, though. When I get enough, I use them to make your Dad pudding."

They still had pudding mix from the move. Rather than ask me to buy them milk, she came up with a more creative and cheaper solution.

ROUGH TALK (8/17/2009)

I was talking to a friend whose mother had Alzheimer's. We were sharing parent stories. He mentioned that his mother was now cursing like a sailor. His comments set me back.

I never focused on the possibility that my mother's recent snide remarks about people and colorful language might be due to her memory loss. Lately I've had to tell her to quiet down and that her comments were not in line with the way she had raised her children. She didn't seem to care in the least. This insensitivity was uncharacteristic of my mother.

During a recent visit, I told her one of her comments was not very nice and might be heard by others. Her answer was quick.

"No one cares. Half of the people here can't hear and the other half can't see and almost everyone can't remember."

After I read more about dementia, I decided that Mom was likely expressing her frustrations and fears through this behavior.

THE MAN (8/25/2009)

Mom could hardly wait to tell me that last night the next-door neighbor, who was in her nineties, knocked on their door at two in the morning. She was shouting there was a man in her room.

Rather than call Security, Dad went to her room to make sure the man was not there. I could just picture Dad walking the halls, clad in his sleeping apparel: a T-shirt and Depends.

Mom said he checked the room, and did not find a man.

Weeks later, my daughter and I were teasing Dad about the incident when Marisa asked what he had done in the woman's room.

He was sitting on his walker and proceeded to get up. Standing up with a smile, he replied. "I dropped my drawers and said here I am." Then he broke out in a loud roar of laughter. We stopped asking him about that night.

86th BIRTHDAY (9/8/2009)

This weekend Jim and I drove to Charleston with Mom and Dad to celebrate Mom's eighty-sixth and her great-granddaughter's third birthdays. We planned on spending a couple of days in Charleston.

Because Dad had a difficult time climbing stairs, my daughter and son-in-law relinquished their first-floor bedroom to my parents.

Mom and Dad were so happy to see everyone. Mom read stories and put puzzles together with her great-granddaughter. Dad played games with her, and I'm not sure who laughed the loudest.

A couple of times over the weekend, confusion set in. We heard voices coming from the bedroom. "Whose house is this?"

Mom thought the messages on the answering machine were for her, so she pressed the play button. We could hear her tell Dad, "Len, the messages must be for you, I don't recognize any of the callers."

The next morning Dad woke up confused. Standing in his T-shirt and diaper, he opened the bedroom door and saw his granddaughter and her husband in the kitchen. He asked why he was in their room. Before they could reply, he woke Mom up telling her they were in the wrong bedroom and needed to pack.

The excitement of the visit really tired them out, and they slept most of the way home. I noticed the more tired Mom got the more confused she became. She must have asked at least a dozen times on the way home what day it was. After the last time she asked about the day, she apologized for not remembering things.

"I hate being like this, forgetting things," she added. "It's really sad to get this way."

I thought. *"It's very sad to see you this way."*

FRIENDS (9/13/2009)

The community where my parents lived was campus-style, containing independent living, assisted living and a nursing home. The assisted living facility was in a separate building.

Since moving to Savannah, Mom and Dad had made many friends. They had seen these people move to the assisted-living facility, move to be closer to family, or pass away. Today, their next-door neighbor moved across the parking lot to the assisted-living facility. Residents were allowed to visit friends in the other buildings but rarely did.

Jim and I had contemplated selling our home and moving closer to Marisa and her family. Jim's son Brian and his family lived in Oregon, and his daughter JoAnn and her family were in Connecticut. Both states were too cold for us. We discussed a move to Charleston near Marisa and Ricardo. They were excited at the idea of having all of us closer.

We loved living on the water, but over time the house and surroundings had become a chore, and we knew it would only get worst. Spending the last two years as my parents' caregiver convinced me that living near your children as you age was important.

The "For Sale" sign went up today. I didn't quite know how my parents would react when they saw the sign.

Mom and Dad came over for the day. Driving past our house, Mom questioned the sign. I explained all our reasons for wanting to move. It didn't seem to bother them in the least. They asked if they would be moving as well. I felt it unfair to force them to move, and I responded by saying that it would be up to them. If they would rather not move, they could stay in Savannah. That was a plastic offer on my part; I had no intention of leaving them in Savannah but was trying to get them to make the decision.

I asked Mom if she would miss her friends if they moved. Her reply was simple and telling. "At our age you don't make friends. You make acquaintances. We're here today and gone tomorrow. We want to be near our family, so moving would be no problem."

Her mind forgets, but it still imparts wisdom.

THE NEWSPAPER (9/23/2009)

I never realized what a good buy the newspaper was until to-day. My Mom had been an avid reader, and still loved to read. She was not into the dime-a-dozen romance novels but read anything she felt was educational: newspapers, magazines, and anything written by Bill O'Reilly, the political commentator, were at the top of her list. When she moved to Savannah, I subscribed to the local newspaper for her, not because she would relate to the local news or read about friends in the obituary column but because it was a good way to re-mind her of the date.

I called her a few times a day to check in, and my first question was usually the same. "What are you doing?"

Her reply was always the same. "I'm reading the newspaper."

We were truly getting value for the dollar with the newspaper subscription. Mom must have read the same articles over and over and over again, and every time it was new to her.

DREAMS (10/20/2009)

Recently Jim and I noticed Dad was slowing down a bit while walking and having a little difficulty getting up from a chair. I was concerned that fluid might be building again on his brain, so I made an appointment with the neurologist.

After waiting the acceptable twenty minutes in the waiting room, a nurse guided Dad and I down the narrow hall to the last ex-amination room on the left. Here we waited another thirty minutes, which was plenty of time to get familiar with our surroundings.

Why do all examination rooms look so morbid? Except for the occasional diplomas hanging on the walls, the eight-by-ten-foot room (I measured with my feet), with its dull beige-gray walls, lino-leum floors, and acoustic tiled ceiling lacked life and was depressing.

At least one bulb was missing in each of the two overhead fluorescent light fixtures. The furniture was old - not antique old but worn-out, cheap old. I believed most people waiting to see a neurologist are depressed enough and would feel better sitting in a brighter room. I was certain neurologists were well paid and could invest a little in making their examination rooms more pleasant.

I tried to make conversation with Dad, but that was difficult to do with a man whose common reply was a nod. After fifteen minutes, I was surprised when out of the blue I heard him talking. "I have some strange dreams."

"What kind of dreams?" I asked.

"I've been dreaming about this dark-haired woman who keeps chasing me."

"Are you sure it's a dream and not one of the ladies in your independent community?" I asked, "Is the lady pretty?"

He laughed and quickly answered, "It's a strange dream and yes, she is pretty."

It was his turn to chuckle when I asked, "Has she caught you yet?"

The doctor finally walked in, shook Dad's hand, asked me how Dad was doing, and exactly one minute later walked out, directing us to the building next door for a CT scan.

We got back in the car, drove next door, and got mentally prepared for waiting once again. That time the wait was much shorter, and the staff was kind and friendly. I helped the technician lift Dad's legs onto the cot and saw the pain in his eyes as she asked him to scoot down to the end of the table.

The room was freezing, and I asked them to cover Dad with a blanket. It was at that moment, I asked God to forgive me for thinking Dad would be happier in heaven. I had begun to pray every night that God grant my parents, when He saw fit, a quick and peaceful death without pain.

A week later we came back for a second CT scan to make sure nothing had changed. Everything checked out fine.

STOCK UP (11/1/2009)

Jim and I were going to Oregon for a week to visit Brian, our daughter-in-law Kelly, and grandson Dylan.

I made sure Mom and Dad's apartment was stocked with everything they would need for a week. Their front closet was stuffed with toilet paper, paper towels, Kleenex, Depends, and soap. They had enough staples for at least a month.

The day before our trip, we picked them up for lunch. I lifted up the seat of my father's walker up to remove the basket. Getting the walkers into the car without the baskets was easier.

Dad the Toilet Paper Hoarder was at it again. Sitting in the basket rolled up was almost a whole roll of toilet paper. I went to check back inside the closet. On the floor were three packages of toilet paper; each contained nine rolls.

HERE WE GO AGAIN (11/14/2009)

I decided to go visit Mom and Dad. On my way I called to let them know I was coming. Mom answered and immediately began to tell me "they" were at it again.

"They took my hair dryer."

As soon as I got to their apartment, I began my hunt for the hair dryer. First I searched the bedroom closet shelf where Mom normally puts it. I was startled as I heard her voice behind me. "See? I told you it was missing."

I searched every place I could think of with no luck as Mom followed me through every room.

Mom used the hair dryer only to dry her shirts after parts of her lunch or dinner landed on her God-given table top. The hair dryer was more than twenty-five years old. It was large and must have weighed at least five pounds.

I kept trying to explain to Mom that no one would want a twenty-five-year-old hair dryer, but she insisted "they" would take anything.

When "they" came to visit, I reverted back to my Catholic up-bringing and prayed to St. Anthony. Call it miraculous or superstitious, but he came through every time. There on the front-hall closet shelf laid the hair dryer. Mom was delighted that I found it, but could not understand why "they" would have put it there.

PILLS, PILLS, and MORE PILLS (12/2/2009)

Ever since the facility started serving breakfast, Mom and Dad rushed downstairs and forgot to take their morning pills.

Without his pills, a friendlier, happier Dad appeared to surface. Jim and I noticed he acted more alert, asking questions and engaging in conversations. Before, he was living on the sidelines and partici-pating only if addressed by name.

The activities director met me in the hall one day and was eager to tell me that Dad got up to dance during the last party. My father loved to dance. I was also approached by several other residents who commented on my Dad's recent sense of humor.

I decided to check on the side effects of his wonder drugs.

He had experienced chest pains in the past and was told he had angina. After researching his medications, I found out that a possible side effect of his heart pill was impaired thinking or delayed reactions.

When I called his doctor and explained the situation, he asked me to monitor Dad's blood pressure and try taking him off the pill. I was uncertain as to whether I made the right decision. I knew I would rather see my father enjoying the last days or years of his life alert rather than in a daze.

MERRY CHRISTMAS (12/23/2009)

Christmas was a big holiday in an Italian household. Family, church, food, fun, and of course a little wine were at the center of the day.

This year my daughter and son-in-law purchased a new home and hoped we would all come for the Christmas holiday. They were looking forward to seeing their three-year-old daughter come down the stairs to see what Santa had brought her.

Thanks to my wonderful husband, the luggage was loaded into the car, and the bicycle rack holding the red and blue rolling walkers was mounted on the back. Jim came up with the brilliant idea of getting a bicycle rack that would hold the walkers. That way it would be easier to access the walkers and allow plenty of room in the back of the SUV for our suitcases and Christmas presents.

Mom and Dad were alert and in high spirits. The drive to Charleston was uneventful except for the periodic "yellow car" spotting and the repeated question of whether we had seen the new house yet.

Marisa and Ricardo had purchased a new mattress and box spring, so Mom and Dad could sleep on the first floor. They converted their office, which was adjacent to a bathroom, into a bedroom for Mom and Dad.

We were blessed to be able to have Mom and Dad with us. They had a great time playing with their great-granddaughter. Dad even got up to dance with her keeping his walker within arm's reach.

Neither one could remember where the bathroom was, even after using it for days. On Christmas Eve, I heard Dad asking Mom, "Where the hell do you pee around here?"

Ricardo had a great idea. He wrote down reminders that would help my parents: you are at Marisa's house; the bathroom is the door to your left; Mariann and Jim are sleeping upstairs. He placed his notes where my parents could easily see them. This made the rest of the visit more relaxing for all of us.

Mom seemed more forgetful and repeated herself frequently, which I attributed to the different surroundings and change of routine. She even came out on Christmas dressed in the same outfit she had worn the day before. When questioned she adamantly replied, "I did not wear this yesterday."

After Jim, Dad, Marisa, and the traces of Christmas Eve dinner reaffirmed that the clothes were worn the day before, she marched to the bedroom and changed.

IS THAT YOU? (12/26/2009)

The day after Christmas we headed back to Savannah. I realized during the drive home that Mom had forgotten most of the Christmas holiday. She did a great job acting when the conversation turned to Christmas, and would say, "Oh, yeah". Obviously she had forgotten almost everything.

After getting them settled back in their apartment, I was very quiet for the rest of the drive home. Jim sensed my sadness. "You have to understand, she really isn't your mother," he said in an attempt to comfort me.

I understood what he was saying, but I disagreed. She was still my mother - not the one I had known and loved my entire life, but a new mother. One who was scared, childlike and dependent. Mom didn't want to forget.

"It bothers me to be like this. I can't remember things. I have half a brain these days," she said often.

I still loved her and prayed for patience and understanding every day so my love didn't turn into bitterness. As the loss of their independence grew daily, their need for me in their lives increased. I was not sure how much of my life I wanted them to take.

NEW YEAR'S EVE (12/31/2009)

Jim and I decided to celebrate New Year's Eve with Mom and Dad at lunchtime. Their facility had a New Year's Eve party, and we had our traditional lobster dinner at home.

Jim bought a bottle of champagne to share with my parents. Mom and Dad were elated to have us there, and Mom, as usual, paraded us around once again, meeting all her friends whose names often slipped her mind.

We sat in the back of the dining room, and Miss E. even brought us a wine bucket to keep the champagne chilled. For some reason, Jim didn't think our inexpensive bottle of champagne would pop when opened. He was wrong. The sound of the cork popping startled everyone in the room. For a minute I feared we would be responsible for causing someone to have a heart attack.

All eyes were focused on our table, and Mom shouted, "Sorry if we bothered you. It was my son-in-law opening the champagne." She had the biggest smile imaginable on her face. She was sipping champagne at noon.

Back in their apartment after lunch, I proceeded to lay out their clothes for the party, the same as my mother had done for me when I was a child.

Later that day I called to make sure they remembered the party. "Mom, are you dressed and do you look beautiful?"

"I look gorgeous. I look so pretty that a man came by and took my picture for the front cover of the community's brochure."

"Mom, really? That's great! When will it be published?"

She went on to tell me she didn't know but her picture would be in it because of the new clothes she was wearing. After about five minutes of me telling her how exciting this was, she without hesitation said, "I fooled you."

Mom's sense of humor had remained intact.

CHAPTER 4
YEAR THREE

CAREGIVER (1/3/2010)

I am a wife, mother, grandmother, daughter, and now caregiver. The latter role was not one that I had ever imagined having or ever really thought about.

All but one of my grandparents died before they reached seventy, and my father's father died of a heart attack at eighty-five. He lived alone and was in good health prior to the day of his death – a heart attack while finishing a piece of pie at the dinner table. I never ever considered that my parents would need my help.

As my parents' caregiver, I found myself filled with conflicting emotions. I loved them and felt blessed to have them still with me. But I must admit, I disliked that they were unable to do simple tasks anymore, like Dad shaving only one side of his face.

I was proud of the way they lived their life but got embarrassed when their food stuck to their lips and clothes. I was happy that they were friendly to everyone, but sad when I got introduced to the same person every time I visited. I felt good when I helped my parents who had done so much for me, but disliked myself when I started to feel resentful.

There was an Italian toast, *cent'anni* which means "one hundred years." We gave this wish on someone's birthday. I'm not certain that living to be a hundred was all that it's cracked up to be.

SHOES (1/9/2010)

I concluded that as you age, you developed a shoe fetish, not a foot fetish.

I couldn't begin to enumerate how many new pairs of shoes I had bought Mom. Since the climate was much warmer here than in Connecticut, sandals were a "must-have." Mom and I shared the same shoe size, so it was easy to buy shoes that would fit her.

She tired quickly these days, so shopping with her was no longer possible. After fifteen minutes, she would be ready to go home. This was sad because Mom had loved to shop, and some of our best times were spent on shopping sprees. She would outlast anyone if bargains were to be found.

I was getting more and more frustrated as she rejected every pair of shoes I bought her.

"I don't like the color. Those shoes are ugly. You paid too much for those."

This went on for months.

One day, Mom happened to mention she thought my sandals were pretty and looked comfortable. Then the light bulb in my head turned on, and the words followed.

"Mom, these aren't my style anymore, and I was going to give them to Goodwill. Would you like them?"

Bingo! I found the solution. I went home and found three other old pairs of shoes and brought them to Mom. She loved all of them.

Dad liked his Rockport shoes. I noticed he had two brand-new pairs in his closet. I asked him why he wasn't wearing them, and the answer was, "I don't know."

I helped him put on the beige pair, which fit perfectly. Next he tried on the black pair. The right foot went in fine, but no matter how hard he tried, the left foot did not fit. I asked him what the problem was, but he sharply replied, "It just doesn't fit."

Several months passed, and I noticed the new shoes sitting in the closet. I was puzzled because they were the same size as all his other shoes. I suggested he try them on again. As previously attempted, the right shoe went on fine but not the left. This time I peeked inside the shoe and pulled out a big wad of stuffing. I was not sure who I believed was dumber - me for not checking the first time, or Dad for not feeling something in the shoe.

EYEGLASSES (1/11/2010)

Our next missing item was Dad's eyeglasses.

I ventured over today to perform my "paper route" delivering toilet paper, paper towels, Kleenex and Depends. I noticed Mom and Dad were at the end of the hall doing chair aerobics. They were finishing up, so I walked down to greet them.

Rather than say hello, Dad greeted me with, "I can't find my glasses."

"They take anything. Who would want your Dad's glasses?" Mom piped up. She read my mind.

I was so proud of myself. My "finding" skills were getting better. I had made this a game to determine how quickly I could find missing items. This time it was less than three minutes. The secret was to look where the item belonged.

They weren't on Dad's head, so I proceeded to the bedroom. I first looked under the bed and then on his night table. They were sitting on the table, half covered by a tissue.

Dad was amazed.

A week later "they" had returned.

I didn't even get the words "Hi, Mom" out of my mouth when she interrupted with, "They took my watch."

I searched all over their apartment in the usual and unusual places where my parents leave things and came up empty handed.

Two days later Mom informed me she had found her watch. That afternoon I went to visit and realized the watch she found was the first watch that "they" had taken. Dad informed me she had found the watch in the pocket of a pair of her pants.

Maybe one day "they" will bring back the other watch.

HAPPY 89th BIRTHDAY (1/21/2010)

Today was Dad's eighty-ninth birthday. His birth certificate had his birth date as 1/20/21, but he had always used 1/21/21. He explained that his mother said the midwife wrote down the wrong date.

I was not sure how he was able to use a birth date that differs from his birth certificate for all these years, but he had, and it had never been a problem.

Dad's birthday happened to fall on the once-a-month birthday celebration night at Savannah Seniors. I thought maybe he might want to celebrate with his friends. I wrestled with whether to go out or celebrate at their place. After much discussion, we decided to go out and had a wonderful birthday dinner.

When we returned, the party was still going on, and the Happy Times trio was playing "When the Saints Go Marching In." Dad walked in on cue. The activities director ran up to Dad and greeted him with a nod toward the dance floor. Dad pulled off his coat, abandoned his walker, and followed her with a spring in his step and a twinkle in his eye to the dance floor.

This was one of the most emotional moments in my life. There was Dad, who months before would not move unless prompted, and now he was dancing. The operation made a difference. This was how I wanted to remember him.

It reminded me of a conversation my brother and I had with Dad on this seventy-eighth birthday. We had all gone to Connecticut to celebrate. My brother and I were up early and in the kitchen watching Dad make coffee. My brother told Dad he looked great and asked him how it felt to be seventy-eight.

"I feel good," he answered.

I asked if he had any pains. I had never forgotten his reply.

"I have the same pains as any other seventy-eight-year old. Every morning I get up and have a choice to make. Either I spend the day thinking about my pains, or I choose to ignore them. I choose to ignore them."

DEATH (1/26/2010)

Today was my "fill the pillbox day." Neither one of my parents could fill their pillboxes anymore. This simple task would take the two of them hours to complete, and they would end up taking the wrong pills or taking too many pills. I knew this because it had happened.

When I got to their apartment, Mom and Dad had returned from chair aerobics. Mom appeared tired. Catching me off guard she questioned, "How do you know when to die?"

"I'm not sure, Mom. Fortunately, I haven't had the experience yet, but I think when a person is ready, their body knows."

She quickly responded, "I think when you're ready, God let's you know. I get so tired these days, sometimes I want to die. I lived a good life for eighty-six years, and maybe I should go soon."

I find it impossible to describe all the emotions I felt as she said these words, but I do know we both felt a moment of spiritual peace. My Catholic upbringing was why I viewed death as a beginning, not an end.

A week later Mom brought up dying again. She must be thinking about it often. "When I die, I don't want you to cry. I want you to say, 'She was ready and lived a good life.' Okay?"

I said "Okay," and wanted to cry, but I couldn't. My tears no longer flowed as quickly as they once did. I had conditioned myself to accept their deaths, and Mom had just asked me not to cry.

FEELING NO PAIN (1/31/2010)

About a week ago, I noticed Mom was favoring her left foot when she walked. She told me nothing was wrong, but I knew better. There on her right toe was a growth the size of a cherry and equally as red.

"Mom, why didn't you tell me?" I asked.

"It doesn't hurt," she replied.

That day we went to the podiatrist.

Mom's memory was getting worse. It was like the movie *Groundhog Day*. She relived the same conversations over and over.

"Where are we going?"

"We're going to see the foot doctor."

Not one stoplight later, she questioned again.

"Where are we going?"

Even when we were sitting in the doctor's office, she asked what doctor we were going to see.

Her toe was infected, but fortunately the infection had not progressed to the bone. The poor doctor was trying to be gentle and poked Mom's toes to see how much sensation she had. She wiggled like a worm and moaned frequently.

She had lost some sensation in her foot, which was why it didn't hurt too much. The doctor explained the importance of her telling me if something like this happened again, pointing out that redness was a sign of infection.

Mom with attitude in her voice responded, "It's red because you're poking around at it. By the way, what's your name?"

The next step was the X-rays. The doctor kindly apologized for having to get Mom up from the chair to stand for the X-rays.

"No problem," she responded. "I'll do anything to get out of here faster."

After three X-rays of the foot, we were done. While the doctor was writing up a prescription, he commented, "She's something else. I think I need the afternoon off."

I added, "Me, too."

Driving home from the doctor's office, Mom shared with me that she could not remember what her apartment looked like. She also could not remember that the podiatrist prescribed her an antibiotic, despite the fact that I explained this to her several times.

I made a chart for the wall to keep track of when the antibiotic needed to be taken. Ten minutes after I hung it on the wall, she forgot what the chart was for.

I find it difficult to imagine what it's like not remembering what you did ten minutes ago.

Mom was also showing signs of frustration. She kept saying, "I hate not having a memory. I really wish I had one."

Oh, how I wished I could give her some of mine.

A week later we took what I hoped was our last trip to the podiatrist. I called twice to remind Mom of her appointment, and she met me outside with a smile.

After getting into the car she asked, "Where are we going?"

"We're going to see the foot doctor."

"That's right. You know I'm forgetting everything lately. My mind is gone."

She whispered this in what was the most serious tone I had ever heard from her. "Do you know who I am?" I replied, trying to make light of what she said.

"Of course. I'll never forget you. You're my precious daughter." How I hoped her words were true.

I thought the doctor actually looked forward to seeing my mother. I was not sure why. Maybe she reminded him of his grandmother. He gave her a big hello and asked us to wait in the first examination room.

Mom took her seat. "I've been here before," she stated with a look of concern.

"Mom, what's the matter?"

"Nothing at all is the matter. As long as I can walk, talk, and eat, I'm happy."

Fortunately the doctor came in before I could think about what she had said and before I started to cry. My emotions were conflicting - sorrow for her memory loss, and admiration for her ability to see life as a gift.

She pointed out her toes to the doctor, and commented on how ugly they were and noted that they were fine. Then she warned him he better say everything was okay and he better not ..., and she made a scissor cutting motion with two of her fingers. He smiled and reassured her he would not be cutting anything, her toe was healing.

As we were walking to my car after the appointment, she said, "Look at the beautiful shiny car."

"Jim washed it and it looks good," I answered.

"Is that your car? Did you just get it? It's beautiful."

I had had my car for four years, and Mom had ridden in it hundreds of times. I used every ounce of energy in my body and, smiled.

I dropped Mom off, and driving home I wanted to cry, but the tears would not flow. All I could do was think about her words: I don't want you to cry when I die.

TAKE YOUR PILLS (2/7/2010)

I called Mom tonight to see if she remembered to take her antibiotics for her foot. I knew the answer before I dialed the phone. I was uncertain as to why I continued to ask futile questions.

"Did you take your foot pill?"

"I don't remember."

I directed her to look on the chart to see if she had checked it off.

"Let me see. Well, no."

"Please take it now."

"Okay, hold on." I could hear her putting down the phone and talking to herself.

"What am I suppose to be doing? Oh, hell, I can't remember." She picked up the phone and asked again,

"What am I suppose to do with this pill?"

This time she listened as I explained. She said "okay," and asked my Dad to pick up the phone and talk to me. In the background I heard her say, "Now what am I suppose to do with this pill, Len? Len look! We didn't take our pills last night. Oh, hell, she can hear me. Okay, I took all my pills. Len, go take your pills."

I could hear him in the background. "They're not in my pill-box. Where are they?"

"Len, look in your hand."

"They're not in my hand," he answered.

"Len, look again."

He quietly replied, "Oh."

This whole exercise took fifteen minutes.

THE EYES HAVE IT (2/16/2010)

Mom and Dad had their annual eye exams today.

This was what I called a "ping-pong visit." I bounced from one room to the other. The ophthalmologist's assistant called Dad in first. I followed him into the examination room and left Mom in the waiting room, reading.

One would think a visit to the eye doctor would be easy. Getting into the chair was the first problem, with trying to manipulate the walker around the equipment. Next was getting Dad to focus on the letters being projected on the small screen in front of him, and not the red lights above. The technician asked Dad four times to read the letters, and four times he said he didn't see any letters. I finally got up and pointed to where the letters were being projected, which helped.

At that point I decided to sneak out to the waiting room, and checked on my mother. She gave me a big smile. I smiled back, mainly because she was reading the same page that she had been reading fifteen minutes before.

When I returned to my Dad, his letter test was over, and he was trying to move toward the slit lamp. Dad could no longer lean forward and keep his chin and his head against the bars on the slit lamp. His head kept leaning backward. After several attempts, the technician called in someone to hold my father's head against the bar.

Now the challenge was to keep his eyes open wide while the technician tried to look into them. She finally gave up and said, "That's enough. The doctor will be in shortly."

That was a good opportunity to bounce back and check on my mother. She was still reading the same page in the waiting room. When she saw me she asked, "What are we here for? I forgot."

Before I could answer, the technician called her into an examination room. I got her settled in the chair. Mom forgot a half-dozen times why she was in the room and kept closing her eyes anytime someone tried to put eye drops in them.

The doctor said Mom had a cataract in her left eye, but nothing needed to be done at the moment.

By the time I returned to Dad, the doctor was with him, trying to get him to lean against the slit lamp. I felt I would save time and got up to help the doctor by holding Dad's head against the bars. When he was finished examining Dad's eyes, he informed me that my father had macular degeneration and asked me how long his sight had been blurry.

"Blurry? Dad, you never told me you're seeing blurry."

"Well, only in my left eye," he said.

The ophthalmologist referred us to a specialist who might be able to help Dad with the macular degeneration.

The following week on the drive to the specialist, Dad burst out, "I slept in the chair last night."

I didn't respond because he dozed off in his chair every night.

"Len, didn't you have chest pains last night?" Mom asked.

"Yeah, that's why I slept in the chair."

"Dad! Why didn't you call and tell me?"

He didn't answer.

I felt guilty and responsible for taking Dad off his heart pills. Since he wasn't having any chest pains at that moment, I decided to stop feeling guilty and focused on the eye problem.

The day was cold and very windy. I dropped Mom and Dad off in front of the building. After getting both of them and their walkers out of the car, I explained twice that the doctor was on the second floor and asked them to wait for me in the foyer.

I parked the car and walked into the building. They were nowhere in sight. I was about to go upstairs but decided to check the first floor waiting room. There they were getting ready to sit down. I realized giving them instructions didn't always work.

We made our way to the second floor, and I filled out more medical forms. I was getting to be an expert on filling out forms and agreeing not to hold anyone liable.

I left Mom with a magazine in the waiting room as Dad and I walked into the examination room. As soon as Dad sat in the chair, he closed his eyes. He looked exhausted. I hated to put him through this, but his sight was important.

Once again a technician tried to get Dad to read the letters. With his left eye he couldn't even read the foot-high letter *E*. When she was done someone else came in and walked Dad into another room for another test. I went to check on Mom.

When I got back, it was off to another room to take some images. I stayed with Dad and had to hold his head against the retinal camera. By that time, he was very tired and had a difficult time keeping his eyes open. I kept asking him if he was all right and if he was feeling any chest pains. His answer was no. We now went back to the first examination room.

I looked into my father's eyes. I would never forget that day. They were as hazel as ever but sad and childlike. I wanted to hold him and tell him everything would be okay.

A third technician entered the room and began with the question, "Did you first notice the blurry vision when you were reading?"

Dad turned toward me with his sad hazel eyes asking me for the answer. I rephrased the question and asked Dad when he first noticed the blurriness.

"I don't remember."

The technician asked the question again and again. Dad's reply was the same. She continued asking the same question. I was getting irritated. I finally replied, "He doesn't remember and doesn't read anymore."

She tried again. "Did you stop reading because of the vision?"

His eyes turned to me again for the answer. I lost it with her continuous questioning, but tried to be calm as I answered.

"He is eighty-nine years old and doesn't read anymore." This time the technician understood the answer, and she left to get the doctor.

Dad's eyes were now closed, and he was ready to sleep. The doctor came in, and once again I helped position Dad's head against the slit lamp.

The doctor proceeded to explain that my father had "wet" macular degeneration. There are two types of macular degeneration, dry and wet. Age-related macular degeneration is the leading cause of blindness in people over fifty years of age.

He then gave us treatment options.

1) Do nothing, but without treatment, vision loss may be quick and severe or

2) Inject a drug called Avastin into the eye. The treatment was to prevent further loss of vision.

I asked if the procedure would be painful. The answer was no, and it would only take a minute to administer. I didn't know what to do. So I asked my usual question.

"What would you do if this was your Dad?"

The doctor immediately replied, "Try to give him the best quality of life, and my eighty-two-year-old Dad is here today to receive the same treatment."

I asked Dad what he wanted to do. He turned looked me in the eyes and said, "Whatever you think is best."

I wanted to shout, *"I don't know what's best anymore!"* Stress was affecting me, and I was getting tired of making decisions for my parents.

I decided to go ahead with the treatment. I felt I needed to do whatever could be done to retain his sight, so he could paint.

At eighty-nine, Dad had started taking art classes at Savannah Seniors - something he'd wanted to do his whole life but never had. I encouraged him to do it and reminded him to go every week. He loved to paint.

After the first injection, the doctor gave me instructions to administer an eye drop that night and four drops a day for the next two days. My initial reaction was selfish: there goes the weekend. I would have to drive to my parents' apartment every three hours, or hire someone to administer the eye drops. Their facility did not provide medication services to independent residents. I did the first drop and went back in the morning to administer the second one.

In the morning, Mom insisted she could do the drops.

"I may look dumb, but I'm not stupid. I won't let you waste your weekend running back and forth."

She did a good job, and I simply needed to call and remind her.

This office visit gave me an idea. I have a suggestion for medical professionals treating the elderly. When someone reaches the age of eighty-five, they should be given priority examinations. Since they did not have many days left in life, it was a shame to waste their time waiting for doctors.

SUNDAY BRUNCH (2/17/2010)

Every other Sunday, brunch was being offered to the residents for free, with a ten-dollar charge for guests. Mom and Dad usually forgot. I had a calendar of their events and called them with a reminder if they were not having breakfast at our house.

That week something unusual occurred. We received a call from my Dad. I was surprised to hear his voice.

"Hi, Mariann, your Mom and I would like to invite you and Jim to brunch this Sunday. We can invite a guest and we would like you to come."

I told him I'd check with Jim and let him know. It took Jim a second to reply. "How can we say no? He never calls!"

All week I kept asking what time we were signed up for brunch and reminding them to make sure they had signed up for two guests. Dad was certain it was at one-thirty, and he was sure he put down two guests.

We arrived a little early so I could do my weekly "fill the pillbox and check things out."

I decided to speak with the hostess. Sure enough, Dad signed up for the one-thirty brunch but failed to include Jim and me. The staff was wonderful and said no problem; they would get a table ready for us.

I was delighted that Dad had invited us, and they were so happy to have had us there.

DON'T BREAK MY HEART (2/28/2010)

When we got home from church, Mom had left a message asking me to call her back. This was rather unusual since it was only nine-thirty in the morning, and Mom rarely called us.

"Your Dad wants to talk to you," she said.

Dad got on the phone and began to tell me he slept in the chair again because he had chest pains. After he had experienced the chest pains a couple of weeks ago, I contacted his doctor and he put Dad back on heart pills. I instructed Dad to take a nitroglycerin pill, and I called the doctor.

The doctor advised if the chest pains continue to bring him into the emergency room. If they went away, he would be fine and requested I contact his office in the morning.

I grabbed my coffee and drove to their apartment. I hated to admit this or sound like a bad daughter, but the last thing I wanted to do was sit in the emergency room all day. I was mentally tired from the eye doctor visit and needed time at home with Jim.

When I got to their apartment, Dad was sitting in his chair. He looked good but said he was still having a little pain. He could not tell me if it was better or worse than the night before. I had no idea how long before the nitroglycerin would take effect, so I decided we should give it another thirty minutes. He had no pain in his left arm – only in the middle of his chest. After thirty minutes, he still said he had chest pains. The hospital was only ten minutes from their home. I decided it would be quicker to drive than call an ambulance. My parents got ready to go, and as we started out the door Dad spoke up: "I don't have any chest pains."

"Are you sure?" I asked.

"Yes, I feel good."

The year before, I took Jim to the emergency room for pains on his left side. We were there more than twenty-four hours getting every inch of him checked out. Knowing how long and tiring the ordeal would be made the decision not to go easy.

It had been three days now, and Dad has had no chest pains.

YOU ARE BLESSED (3/9/2010)

Today was my parents' six-month checkup with their doctor. Last week they got their blood tests, and this week we received the results. The appointment was for ten-thirty in the morning. I called at nine to start the reminder process. I reminded them the night before that we were going to the doctor's office, but I had learned, one reminder was no longer enough.

Dad answered the phone.

"Hi, Pop. Have you eaten breakfast?"

"No, we haven't eaten yet."

"Well, why don't you and Mom go downstairs for breakfast, and bring your coats with you. I'll pick you up at ten outside."

I had him repeat what I said out loud so Mom would hear it, too. At nine-thirty, before leaving the house, I called again.

Mom answered. "Hi, Mom, are you all ready to go?"

"Well, almost. Can we eat breakfast?"

Once again, I repeated the words given to Dad.

At ten, I drove up to the front door looking for them. They were in the lounge area leisurely finishing up their coffee. So much for reminders!

The minute Mom got in the car she began to talk. "You know I can't find my watch. They take everything. Someday when you're in a store, would you buy me a new one? Make it cheap."

I felt like I was the ringmaster of a three-ring circus when we go to the doctor's office. It was I pointing out the way, followed by Mom. In the rear was Dad. They took a seat while I checked them in.

When I sat down, Mom said, "Look at your father's shiny head. Isn't it nice?"

Several people around us gave a smile. She proceeded to ask me why she and Dad were there and if she was going to get weighed. Then she announced she only eats what was put in front of her and never ate anything unhealthy. Dad gave her a challenging look and started to laugh. Then Mom and I started to laugh, and so did the couple sitting behind us.

She turned around and in a childlike way asked the man if he was laughing at her.

"No, I'm laughing with you," he quickly replied.

She proceeded to confide in him that I believed she was eating too much and went on to tell him all about herself. When we were called in for our appointments, she waved goodbye to the couple. The gentleman thanked Mom for giving him something to smile about.

Mom was the first to get examined. Months before, she tipped the scales at 151 pounds. I could tell she had gained more weight and was not looking forward to finding out how much. The nurse helped Mom onto the scale, and I thought she was going to jump off when the scale tipped at 162 pounds. I could hardly believe what I was seeing. Mom now weighed more than Dad. Sixty-two years ago when Mom and Dad were married, she was 102 pounds.

"Your scale is wrong. I still have my shoes on, and my shirt is heavy."

The nurse reassured her not to worry she would subtract four pounds for clothes. After the nurse left the room, Mom shouted, "My bra weighs at least three pounds! She did not take that into account."

Other than the weight, both examinations went well.

I was in line waiting to check out at the doctor's office when the woman in front of me turned around.

"Are you the daughter of the cute older couple in the waiting room?"

"Yes."

With a smile, she responded, "You are blessed."

Running through my mind was: Yes, *but I am also tired and I hate to admit this, slightly angry that I have this responsibility interfering with my life.* I was not proud of the latter feeling. I wished my brother lived closer to share some of the responsibility. This was not how Jim and I had planned our retirement.

When we got back to my parents' building, two women were in the elevator as we approached. One immediately said, "You'll have to wait for the next elevator." She quickly pressed the button to close the elevator door. Mom stuck her walker in the door.

"There is plenty of room for us," Mom said as she proceeded inside.

I'm not sure why the woman did that. She did not look pleased as we entered the elevator.

To break the ice, I asked the ladies if they had been outside enjoying the beautiful day. The woman who didn't want to share the elevator answered. "Yes, but it isn't very nice outside. It's too cold and breezy."

At that moment I felt blessed again. Mom and Dad never complained about anything. They were so easy to please and appreciative of every day. For as long as I could remember, my mother started every morning thanking God for allowing her to see another beautiful day.

I was almost ready to leave their apartment when Mom reminded me that "they" took her watch.

I was astonished. After a quick prayer to St. Anthony, I found both missing watches. One was in the pocket of the slacks Mom had worn the day before. The other watch, the one that disappeared months ago, was in her dresser in a small jewelry box. I was not sure what led me to look there, but that's where "they" put it. I gave St. Anthony full credit and thanks.

TIME DOESN'T MATTER (3/14/2010)

Driving Mom and Dad over to our house for breakfast, I asked them if they had set their clocks back to Eastern Standard Time.

"I have to remember everything, and I remember nothing," Mom replied.

Even simple tasks are difficult for them to complete, such as, changing the time on their watches and clocks, replacing the TV remote control batteries, and tying their shoes.

Jim made his usual delicious pecan and blueberry pancakes, which we all enjoyed so much.

Driving home after bringing my parents back to their apartment, I came to the realization that it didn't matter anymore if we spent an hour or a day or a week with my parents. What matters was that we were with them. They were delighted to have, as Mom expressed it, "a change of scenery."

These days, I saw so many lonely people at my parents' residence just waiting to die. They got so excited by a simple hello and a minute or two of conversation to break up their routine and boring day. It was sad that people often tend to ignore the old. I think people find it difficult to see their loved ones age, so they avoid the situation. Folks living in the same senior apartments as my parents had children in town and saw them once a month. How sad for all of them.

A LOVE AFFAIR (3/21/2010)

Returning home from a trip to Home Depot, Jim suggested we stop in to see Mom and Dad.

We were all sitting in their living room when Mom whispered, "I have a secret."

"Really? What is it?" Jim asked.

"Well, I'm not sure I am supposed to tell you, but I will. Pop has a girlfriend."

Jim and I looked at each other, startled, and did all we could not to fall off our chairs with laughter.

"Pop, you have a girlfriend?" I questioned.

"Oh, yes, it's Marge. She and I love each other." He said the word love rolling back his tongue on the "lo" for a long time.

"Mom, is this your friend Marge?"

"Yes, my best friend, Marge." Then she and Dad turned toward each other and smiled.

A week later I stopped in while Mom was getting her hair done. The hairdresser seemed anxious to talk to me.

"Have you heard about your Dad and Marge? They act like they are having an affair."

Not that I wanted to imagine it, but I could not even visualize what an affair was between two almost ninety-year-olds, but at this point let them dream.

The hairdresser proceeded to tell me, "I think your Mom is in on the rumor, too."

Weeks later I found out that Marge's son wanted to move her to assisted living, and she was opposed to the change. It appeared that several residents were in on a plot to demonstrate how unhappy Marge would be living elsewhere without her friends. I believe Dad was part of the conspiracy.

THE EYES HAVE IT (3/24/2010)

We returned to the eye doctor's office for another treatment to inject Avastin into Dad's eye. Mom was getting her hair washed and set, it was only Dad and me.

The waiting room was packed, but our wait was rather short. We must have gotten lucky.

Dad's vision had not changed, so the doctor decided to try one more treatment.

Later in the day I called to remind my mother to give Dad his eye drops. She replied in a loving voice, "I feel so sorry for you having to take care of two *senapismo*."

The word she used was Italian for, "mustard plasters." I asked what she meant.

"Well, you know, mustard plasters are heavy on your chest and smell bad."

I assured her that they had not started to smell yet!

I WANT MY PARENTS TO BE COOL (4/10/2010)

My daughter and her family came to visit this weekend. I picked Mom and Dad up, so they could spend time with their granddaughter and great-granddaughter.

A visit with young children was uplifting to older people. I had noticed how an elderly person's eyes change from sad and droopy to happy and bright when they were around young children and small dogs. Mom and Dad had happy eyes. They even pushed their walkers faster toward the car.

As I helped Dad into the car, I could not help but notice a stain in the front of his pants. Oh, hell, I thought. I hoped he was not losing bladder control. I was not sure how long he had been wearing those pants and wondered if the stain was a remnant from a soup spilled at dinner. He didn't see the stain or seem to care when I asked him about it. I ran up to their apartment, and got a clean pair of pants for him to change into at to my house.

I found that Dad, like many older people, would wear the same clothes day after day. He had been pretty good about changing his clothes up until now.

It didn't seem to matter to my parents anymore if stains appear on their pants in embarrassing locations, or on their shirts.

I was constantly trying to make my parents look good. I guess even at their age and mine, I didn't want my parents to be talked about and ostracized by the other residents. For them to continue living independently, they would have to start caring about how they dressed.

I read in an issue of the AARP Bulletin that older adults could be bullies. The article stated that between ten and twenty percent of residents in senior care homes were mistreated by peers. I saw no signs that my parents were being bullied but feared their appearance might trigger this to happen.

My parents didn't seem to care, but it was hard for me not to care. It was similar to raising your children and wanting them to be the kid everyone liked and didn't tease.

When I brought my parents home, I went up and gathered all of Dad's pants and took them home to wash.

The next day, I stopped by their apartment with six pair of clean pants. I handed them to Mom and asked that she put them away.

STAINS (4/20/2010)

It's been a week since I've seen Mom and Dad. Today Dad had another eye doctor's appointment.

As I pulled up to their building, they were walking out. They were happy to see me, and I was happy to see them. My attitude changed as Dad approached me. He was wearing what appeared to be the remains from last night's dinner, spaghetti sauce, on the front of his pants. He had no time to change, so I helped him get into the car and requested he pull down his sweater. Since he was short, this helped cover some of the spaghetti sauce.

"Dad, do you realize your pants are stained?"

He gave me a puzzled look. "I don't have any other pants."

"What do you mean? I left you six clean pair last week. Have you checked in your closet?"

"I'm not sure," he replied.

I was so frustrated. Now I questioned my mother. "Mom, didn't you see that Dad's pants are stained?"

"It's not my job to keep track of him. I have enough problems keeping track of myself."

Mom had a good point, and I was not going to resolve this now. My mind was focused on the doctor visit.

I was getting used to the smiling faces that pass us as we paraded into the doctor's office. Mom always stopped to make sure Dad was close behind, and I heard her say, "Come on, father, this way."

I was grateful to all these strangers for the kind smiles. Often they were all the encouragement I needed to get through the day.

The waiting room was full, and we waited more than an hour before we got to see the doctor.

The treatments had not helped Dad's eyes. His vision with glasses was 20/40 in the right eye and 20/400 in the left.

I didn't understand how he could lose his sight and not tell anyone. It had to have happened within the year, since they have their eyes examined once a year. Then I realized he may have shared his problem with Mom, but she would not have remembered.

The doctor recommended we return in four months and let him know if the vision in the right eye changed. It was hard for me to stay composed. How would I handle caring for a father that could not see?

When I was back in their apartment, my attention shifted from eyes to pants. I had to find his pants. I looked through his side of the closet, in the front-hall closet, and in the spare-room closet. No pants. Now I was really frustrated. I went back to their bedroom closet but this time looked on Mom's side. There they were, hanging in the middle of her clothes.

When I told them where I found the pants, mom quickly had an answer. "Well, you can't blame your father for not finding his pants when they were mixed in with my clothes."

She had no idea she was the one that put them there.

I didn't want these people. I want my real parents back: the ones who gave me advice, solicited and unsolicited, not these people who look at me with sad eyes searching for answers I didn't have.

IN GOOD COMPANY (4/22/2010)

I read today in the AARP Bulletin that the number of unpaid family caregivers in the United States tops sixty-five million, and one-third of them are men. The article stated that women tend to be more hands-on than men, but I was sure whether a man or woman, the job was no easier. We all shared the same emotions of love, guilt, frustration, doubt, fear, embarrassment, and at times, despair.

On the other hand, I was certain non-caregivers experience some of the same emotions, but being removed from the situation on a daily basis allowed one to imagine things better than they were. It is important that non-caregivers understand that caregivers need help.

I had a conversation with a friend whose brother was the primary caregiver for their ninety-seven-year-old mother. He lived in the same town as their mother and she lived hundreds of miles away. She visited her mother often and did as much as she could to help. I admitted to her that what I needed the most as the caregiver was a "thank you." She acknowledged that she never thought to thank her brother.

My brother called today to see how I was doing. My sister-in-law, Marie, called yesterday to check on me.

I was happy to hear from both of them and welcomed their concern. Simple gestures like that made me feel appreciated.

My brother and sister-in-law still worked. Lenny called our parents daily. He was very appreciative and supportive, and he trusted me to make all decisions, both financial and medical, for my parents. For this I was grateful, I had several friends who had to get "sibling consensus" before any decisions were made, especially where finances were concerned.

My brother also tried to plan his visits around times that Jim and I were on vacation, so someone was here for my parents.

YESTERDAY (5/9/2010)

This was Mother's Day weekend. My daughter, son-in-law, and granddaughter came for the weekend.

On Saturday, Marisa and I picked up Mom and Dad for the afternoon, and I prepared an Italian dinner my grandmother would be proud of. Dad took a nap before dinner, but Mom was not going to miss a minute with her family. It was warm enough to go in the pool, and Mom thoroughly enjoyed watching her three-year-old great-granddaughter kicking and splashing in the water. Mom was energized by all the activity.

When Dad woke up, he came outside without waiting for us to unfold his walker and quickly went toward his great-granddaughter for a kiss.

My parents were both tired and happy by the end of the day. We planned to have brunch with them on Sunday at their place and reminded them a dozen times.

Sunday morning I called to wish Mom a Happy Mother's Day. She was thrilled to hear from me and got very excited when I said we were coming for brunch. She asked several times who was coming and if I had notified the kitchen staff. My answer was always the same, but I answered as if it were the first time I'd heard the question.

My husband was amazed that I could talk to my mother without getting frustrated. I treated her like I did before all her memory problems. I explained to Jim that she was still my mother, I still loved her, and she didn't want to be like this, so why would I want to treat her any differently?

We had a wonderful brunch. Both Mom and Dad were happy to walk with us around the dining room, showing us off to all their friends. Mom especially enjoyed doing this and introduced us over and over to the same people.

During brunch, I asked her if she enjoyed dinner yesterday. She gave me a blank expression. "Dinner? I forgot where we ate dinner."

"Remember? You came over, and I made an Italian dinner for you."

She paused. "Oh, yes, we had a great time."

It was then that I recognized Mom had become a very good actress. She had spent seven hours with us the day before, and I was not sure she remembered any of it. I could not imagine what it was like to have no memory. Thank God she still knew her family. She had started to refer to us as "her people."

Brunch was accompanied by a pleasant woman who played the piano. I felt today she played the most appropriate song as my family walked out of the dining room in a procession. The tune was "Yesterday" by the Beatles. The words from the song kept repeating in my mind. *"Yesterday, all my troubles seemed so far away. Now it looks as though they're here to stay. Oh, I believe in yesterday. Suddenly, I'm not half the man I used to be. There's a shadow hanging over me. Oh, yesterday came suddenly."*

How I wished Mom could have a yesterday again. Now, her yesterdays go suddenly.

A THING OF THE PAST (5/1/2010)

Mom consistently provided good advice. I, on the other hand, did not always listen or take her advice.

One bit of advice, I clearly remembered was on how she and my Dad stayed happily married for all these years. Her answer was simple and important for any aspect of life. "No shouldas, couldas or wouldas." I decided to ignore that advice now in hopes others might learn from my experience.

I *shoulda* asked them more questions about their lives and our family history when they *coulda* remembered and *woulda* loved to share them with me.

Today, I've finally admitted to myself that I could no longer ask my parents questions about the past. I had tried, but the attempt disappointed all of us.

I NEED A HUG (5/12/2010)

Recently a young and strong man who attended our church died after fighting cancer for two years. He was fifty-six and too young to die.

At fifty-nine, mortality was becoming a factor in my life. I had a desire to complete a bucket list like in the movie, but my list wasn't as extraordinary.

This year, I decided to start checking things off the list, such as making a gingerbread house with my granddaughter, and attending an Easter sunrise service on the beach.

I had traveled all over the world: China, Europe, Africa, and Australia, but had never seen the Grand Canyon, Yellowstone, Mt. Rushmore and other parts of the United States. Seeing these American treasures had been a bucket-list item of mine. Jim and I decided this would be a good time to do it before my expectant daughter had our new grandson, and while my parents were still in reasonably good health. We planned to be away for almost four weeks, stopping to visit Jim's son and family in Oregon along the way.

I explained to Mom and Dad that Jim and I would be back soon, and they could use the cell phone to call us anytime. I reassured them I would call often. I had been working weeks to get Mom and Dad's needs met before the trip. I took them to the doctor's for a physical, filled their prescriptions, cut Dad's nails and hair, stocked their closet with paper products, and notified the independent-living management and friends of our departure.

My brother agreed to visit while we were away.

We planned to leave on Saturday, so on Friday I dropped off linens and a pillow for my brother. Mom and Dad had a single bed in their spare room. Lenny enjoyed staying with them when we traveled.

My parents greeted me with huge smiles. Mom held up a Mother's Day present from my granddaughter. It was a dishtowel my granddaughter had painted for her in school.

"What is this?" Mom asked.

"A Mother's Day present from Isabella."

Then it happened.

"Oh, I'll save it for when I go back home."

Both my Dad and I stared at her, not believing what we had heard. Dad responded, since I was still in shock. "You are home. We are not going back to Connecticut."

"What do you mean? We're never going back to Humphrey Street?"

By this time I had composed myself. "No, Mom, you live here now."

I knew this day would happen but hoped and prayed it never would. My husband and friends had warned me about this moment, but until I experienced it myself, I didn't understand. It was like someone tore out my heart, and relocated it to my stomach. I wanted to shout to all children who still have parents, *Call them, listen and talk to them, and hug them while you still can!*

Leaving Mom and Dad for such a long period of time concerned me. I knew anxiety was not good for people suffering from dementia and Alzheimer's disease. I had also learned that no matter what you do to ease the anxiety in a loved one, it is still there, but I couldn't blame myself for being a little selfish and working on my bucket list. My only hope was that tomorrow Mom would be better.

AMERICA THE BEAUTIFUL (5/22/2010)

Lenny arrived to stay with my parents on Friday, and I was very happy he was there.

Jim and I were a week into a wonderful cross-country trip when Mom developed what seemed at first to be a normal cold or more likely a sinus problem.

When she was no better on Sunday, I asked Lenny to take her to the doctor's for a checkup the next day. From past experience I understood that an elderly person's simple cold could turn to something worse.

On Monday, I called and made an appointment for her to see the doctor. The doctor's nurse and I had a good relationship, and I knew if I called, Mom would be seen that day. I gave my brother the doctor's phone number and directions to his office.

I was anxious to hear from my brother, and hoping that Mom was okay. I called early in the afternoon to find out what the doctor had to say.

"Mom said she was feeling better and didn't think she needed to see the doctor," he explained.

I had always loved and respected my brother, but for the first time in my life I wanted to strangle him. I knew he sensed my aggravation. I was upset. I reasoned with myself that he probably was torn between listening to me and listening to his mother, whom he had always obeyed. His flight to return home was the next day.

I prayed Mom would get better, but as the week progressed, she developed a cough. She continued to say, "I'm fine. Don't worry."

MEMORIAL DAY WEEKEND (5/30/2010)

Halfway through our trip, on the Sunday before Memorial Day, while on the West Coast visiting Brian, Kelly and Dylan, my cell phone rang. The activities director at my parents' residence was calling. My heart skipped several beats. She noticed Mom had developed a bad cough and suggested she see a doctor if I could arrange it.

Being almost three thousand miles away, it took numerous calls and the help of our doctor's wonderful nurse to get an appointment to see the doctor on Tuesday.

A good friend of mine agreed to accompany Mom. She was an angel, staying with Mom during the checkup and several tests. Helping my mother remove and re-hook her bra during the examination and tests went way beyond friendship.

The day was hot. My friend told me Dad patiently sat in the waiting area, and he started to sing, "Let it snow, let it snow, let it snow" whenever she went to check on him.

The doctor diagnosed a bacterial infection. He also sent Mom to get an echocardiogram. She had been having problems breathing lately, which we had been attributing to her weight gain. The echocardiogram uncovered a small blockage in one artery but nothing that could not wait until we returned home.

Jim and I were feeling better now that Mom had seen a doctor and was on medication.

Our enthusiasm was soon to be crushed. Several days later, Mom complained that her ribs ached, and the pain was worse than anything she had experienced before. My mother had never been one to complain, so I knew she was really hurting.

A HELPING HAND (6/8/2010)

We shortened our trip, and returned home in three days. Over-the-counter pain medication provided Mom with relief until we got home.

Within an hour of getting back in town, we were waiting for Mom's turn to get X-rayed.

The young woman technician asked Mom to undress from the waist up and put on the stylish blue paper coat. I helped Mom remove her shirt and her bra. I decided it would be best to tie the coat in the back, so neither "girl" would accidentally sneak out.

The technician had Mom stand in front of the X-ray machine, and she repeatedly tried to get an X-ray of my mother's ribs. Each X-ray was to some degree blocked. The technician found it difficult to get a clear picture of her ribs because as the technician explained, "The breast tissue is in the way."

A second technician entered the room to help. I soon found out that my next statement was a mistake.

"Is there anything I can do to help?"

"Well, if we could lift her breasts up and over to one side, we might be able to get a better image. Would that be okay?"

They weren't my breasts, so I asked Mom the question.

"If it gets me out of here faster, do whatever you need to," was her sharp reply.

At that point I wanted to retract my offer to help. Looking directly at me the technician said, "If you don't mind putting on the lead jacket, maybe you would be the best one to lift your mother's breasts."

Oh, what the heck, if I could see Dad's manly parts, I could lift a breast or two. Dressed in a lead jacket that came to my knees and weighed more than I did, I was ready for the task ahead. I stood next to Mom and awaited my instructions. Both technicians were in a serious conversation trying to analyze how to accomplish the task at hand.

A few minutes passed before one of them said, "You need to be on the other side of your mother."

I smiled and replied, "How am I going to manage that? The machine is in the way."

"Well, if you can get on the floor and come in front of your mother that should work."

At first I thought she was kidding, but I quickly understood how serious she was. So there I was crawling in this heavy lead coat on the floor between my mother and the X-ray machine.

"Now try to reach and lift up your mother's breast, and push it over," the technician directed.

I couldn't help myself and started to laugh. I was laughing so hard I almost peed on the floor. It was either laugh or cry. I glanced up at Mom and asked if she had a problem with me doing this.

"Do whatever the hell you need to, so we can get out of here," she sharply answered.

"I don't think this will work. You can get up now." The technician said after two failed attempts.

My only regret was that I didn't have them take a picture of this unbelievable episode.

It turned out that Mom had a minimally displaced tenth rib likely caused by her coughing. I was not sure if it was the ibuprofen or our return home that helped Mom get better.

I'M NOT READY FOR ASSISTED LIVING (6/12/2010)

A lovely couple had lived across the hall from my parents for two years. The husband was very frail looking and passed away about six months ago. His wife recently moved to be closer to her children. Their apartment was a one-bedroom with a nice covered balcony overlooking the entrance to the building and had sunlight for most of the day.

Mom and Dad's apartment was a two-bedroom without a balcony and on the dark side of the building. I decided it would be great to move them across the hall. They rarely used the second bedroom except when my brother visited, and he could stay at my house. It would be good for them to have an outside balcony to sit on.

Even though we had our house on the market, Jim and I had no idea how long it would take to sell. Moving my parents across the hall would be easy and much better for them.

The apartment was available, and the manager informed me Mom and Dad could move in anytime.

A good friend who had experienced caregiving to both her mother and mother-in-law asked, "Do you think they might be ready for assisted living?"

Hearing the words made me edgy. I had read nightmarish stories about neglect and abuse in assisted-living facilities, and the effect it had on both the person living there and their caregivers.

Another friend told me she had received a call one night from a staff member who had overheard her ninety-five-year-old mother planning to escape from her assisted-living facility. That night her mother called repeatedly announcing she "wanted out of the facility." My friend stopped answering the phone, but her persistent mother kept leaving messages – twenty-two in total.

I wrestled long and hard with the decision, asking the opinion of a trusted staff member at my parent's facility. She shared that Mom and Dad were doing much better than some residents.

The best advice I received was from a friend who told me to do what made me feel better. To me, sending my parents to an assisted-living facility would be a daily reminder that their life was over. I knew the day was not far off in the future, but I was determined to prolong their independence as long as possible. Emotionally, I was not ready to accept that my parents needed assisted living.

Thanks to the help of great friends, the move across the hall only took a day. My parents adjusted immediately to their new surroundings, and sadly, after two days Mom forgot what the other apartment looked like.

The layout of the new apartment was the reverse of their old apartment, less the one room. For almost sixty years Dad had slept on the left side of the bed and Mom on the right. The day after the move I noticed his glasses on the right night table.

"Dad, what side of the bed do you sleep on?" I asked.

Mom was quick to answer for him. "Dad sleeps near the bathroom, so he has always slept on the right side."

Like children, they adapted to the change with ease.

FATHER'S DAY (6/20/10)

Mom and Dad came for brunch to celebrate Father's Day.

I couldn't believe the change in my father. He had become the one in charge.

Mom was becoming more and more dependent on him, relying on him to remember everything: what time they eat, when they need to do laundry, and where they go for activities. She now depended on him for the answers to questions.

I was showing them some pictures of Jim and me taken on a recent visit to see our grandchildren in Connecticut.

"Do you recognize anyone in the picture?" I asked smiling.

"Of course. That's my beautiful daughter and her handsome husband," Dad replied with a big grin.

Dad was quiet and not a conversationalist. He was now making up for what Mom couldn't do. He was becoming the strong one. Dad had assumed his new role without question, and did what was necessary to help his wife. That was true love and devotion.

MOM'S TURN (7/13/2010)

Jim and I had just finished applying the first coat of paint in our dining room and decided to break for lunch when the phone rang. We inevitably tackled projects, when we were ready to sell a home, which we had wanted to address for years.

It was my Dad. He rarely called. When I heard his voice, I knew something was wrong.

"Mariann, your mother can't get up from the chair."

"What's wrong, Dad?"

"She has pains in her ribs and can't move."

I told him we would be right over.

Jim and I jumped out of our paint clothes, dressed, and drove to their apartment. We found Mom slouched in the most uncomfortable-looking position in her chair. She appeared to be in a lot of pain, and we immediately called 911.

An ambulance arrived quickly.

Mom was only wearing a nightgown. She was very self-conscious ... she did not have anything on underneath the gown.

The emergency medical technicians (EMTs) were wonderful. They treated Mom with dignity, respect, and kindness. I could not say enough about these unrecognized heroes. They gently lifted her from the chair and onto the stretcher.

As we left her apartment, Mom turned toward me. "Am I going to die today?"

I was taken aback at first but replied, "Not if you don't want to."

"I don't want to, not today," she answered.

When we arrived at the hospital, the emergency room was crowded. Mom was assigned to Hall 2 which was the space in the hall in front of Room 2. Mom said goodbye to the technicians, telling the younger one he was cute and had a nice smile. Then she turned to the older one. "You are very nice, too."

We spent six and a half hours in our makeshift "room" through several tests and the arrival and departure of numerous patients.

Dad rode over with Jim and was sitting in the waiting room. After four hours, Jim offered to take Dad home so he could rest and have dinner. Dad wanted to see Mom and say goodbye before he left. I walked with him into the emergency room, reassuring him, that Mom would be fine. They smiled at each other, and Mom was first to talk.

"Len, have you eaten? You must be hungry."

"I had lunch. I love you." He leaned closer and gave her a kiss.

I was moved by the concern and love they expressed for each other, and so proud that these people were my parents.

The tests ruled out heart issues and broken ribs. The doctor explained Mom could not be admitted without cause, so she would be discharged and was allowed to go home. As calmly as I could I repeated the words much louder than the doctor.

"Go home? How am I going to accomplish that when she can't even stand up without pain?"

He gave me a puzzled look and went to talk with the nurse. She came back and informed me that Mom was going on a morphine drip to help with the pain.

After a half hour, the nurse notified me I could take Mom home. I informed her if she could get Mom to stand up, I would be happy to take her home. She tried to raise Mom's head and attempted to get her to sit up. Instantly, Mom cried out with pain. The nurse gave me a bewildered look and went to speak with the doctor.

I called Jim and explained the situation. I tried to instruct him and my father where to find clothes and shoes for my mother. This took ten minutes.

I managed to smile when Jim arrived with her clothes in a white kitchen trash bag.

The nurse returned and handed Mom two pills and water. About a half hour later we were able to get Mom up. She was feeling no pain. As I was helping her, I realized the back of her nightgown was wet. It must have happened during the last bedpan exercise. I asked if someone on staff could help me get her dressed. The nurse at the desk suggested I take Mom home in her nightgown. Sure, with no underwear and a large wet pee spot in the back of her nightgown – no way. She deserved to be treated with respect.

Mom and I were led to the bathroom and offered a washcloth and towel. I wasn't sure how I would be able to find the strength, but I believed God was with me.

I got her out of the wet nightgown, and quickly washed and dressed her. We left with three prescriptions.

After buying Mom a Chick-fil-A sandwich and filling the prescriptions, we headed to Savannah Seniors. I called Dad and told him we were on our way.

What happened next makes me smile and cry every time I recall the moment. Dad was walking toward us as we exited the elevator. With a look on his face that reminded me of a child on Christmas morning, he shouted out, "Sweetheart, I missed you. I'm so happy you're home. I love you." Mom quickly answered back, "I love you too, Len."

I helped Mom put on a clean nightgown and a Depends, just in case. She insisted on brushing her teeth, and I gave her two of the pills as directed. She said she wasn't tired, felt fine, and would call if they needed any help.

WHERE IS MOMMA? (7/14/2010)

I called first thing in the morning. Dad answered and said Mom was sitting in her chair, in her nightgown. He had gotten her breakfast and given her a pill. Hearing her in the background, I knew she was still in pain, and I felt concerned as to what pill Dad had given her. I learned to count the number of pills left in the bottles to determine how many had been taken.

Before leaving the emergency room, the doctor mentioned that my mother's doctor would probably want to check her out. I left a message for her doctor and headed over to see Mom.

There I found Mom slouched in the same position as the day before. I needed to get her washed and dressed in case the doctor wanted to see her. After some convincing, I was able to maneuver her into the shower chair. She seemed okay. She helped as best she could and in five minutes we soaped and rinsed. Any attempt to describe what it was like to give my Mom a shower would be futile. I couldn't say I was getting used to the sight of her naked. I did what I had to do, and developed the same attitude as a medical professional. It was no big deal anymore.

Once again I helped her get dressed, and then I checked the pills. Dad had given her one of the three prescriptions. Thinking I was doing the right thing, I handed her a glass of water and the other pills. Fifteen minutes later, Mom was dozing.

When awake, her speech was slurred and her conversation incoherent. She asked my Dad where Momma was. She was referring to her mother who passed away forty-five years ago.

He looked at me as if to say, what should I tell her?

"Your Mom died and is in heaven," I explained.

She was mortified and fell back to sleep. At one point she announced, "I need to go to the bathroom."

She was already standing when I went to help her into the bathroom. Before I realized it, she had fallen. She was so incoherent, she gazed up at me and said, "What am I doing down here? I think I need to go to the bathroom."

I wanted to cry.

She then said, "I love you, and don't worry, I think I'm going to die soon." Then she fell back to sleep on the floor.

I called the front desk for help and was informed due to liability concerns the staff was no longer allowed to help lift residents in the independent-living facility. The receptionist offered to call 911. I called Jim for help, and he came right over.

Several staff members stopped in to explain the best method for getting Mom up. Somehow we were able to lift her or should I say somehow Jim was able to lift her. That was surprising, considering Jim weighed less than Mom.

I immediately called the doctor. He took Mom off all the medications, and said if she was not better in the morning to bring her in. The doctor's nurse informed me that using Ativan together with Citalopram may increase side effects such as dizziness, drowsiness, and difficulty concentrating. Mom was already taking Citalopram to prevent depression that could result from her dementia. I was confused why the emergency room doctor would also prescribe Ativan.

I stayed with my parents all day. I sat listening to Mom purr in one chair and Dad honk in the other. They were clueless as to my presence. I wondered what it was like to be old and not in control of your life.

I got Mom ready for bed before I left. I arranged to have someone on staff get her into bed and check on her throughout the night.

The next day she had no recollection of the day before. She was a little weak but managed to go down for dinner.

BREAKFAST (7/24/2010)

It had been ten days since Mom's fall and she was herself again. I called my parents to ask them out for breakfast tomorrow. They were both delighted and said yes instantly. I arranged to call them the following morning at nine to set up a pickup time.

The following morning, I called at nine. No answer. I kept trying for twenty minutes. Then I decided to call the front desk. I asked the receptionist, if she had seen Mom and Dad this morning.

"Yes, they're eating breakfast."

"I made plans to take them out for breakfast." I must have sounded disappointed because she quickly added, "It's just their usual light breakfast, a Danish pastry. You can still take them to breakfast."

Knowing my parents, they were eating more than one Danish pastry. I decided to do breakfast another time.

My daughter called later that morning and I explained what happened. She shared some good advice.

"Mom, stop feeling so bad. It's irrelevant to them. They love going to breakfast, but they may or may not remember having gone. They're happy."

I knew she was right.

Later that day Jim and I stopped by to see them. We had gotten a new battery for Dad's watch. Dad had reminded me a dozen times about the battery. *That*, he could remember!

In conversation, I turned to Mom and said, "Sorry we missed taking you to breakfast this morning."

She quickly turned to Dad. "Len, did we have breakfast this morning? Where did we eat it?"

Dad gave her a bewildered look. "I don't know."

WE'RE NOT BORED (7/28/2010)

I thought the worst thing for the elderly was to sit around and watch TV all day long. I had friends whose parents did that by choice. I believed one of the secrets to a long, happy life was to keep active.

One of Mom's favorite activities was arts and crafts. She would forget my visiting her, but she could rattle off everything she had made: the Popsicle stick basket, the wooden tray with glued-on flowers, the clay pot wind chime, the ceramic hot plate, the paper-clip bookmark, and the plate with flowers. She wanted me to have everything she made. I accepted these gifts with enthusiasm and pride.

I remembered, as a child, making potholders, leather wallets, and beaded necklaces, and presenting these wonderful gifts to my parents. They acted pleased when I offered them one of my creations.

The roles had switched, and I was the one receiving the not so perfectly made items. I had come to the point in my life when material things were becoming less and less important, but these gifts I would cherish forever.

Beside arts and crafts, Mom loved Bingo, and she rarely forgot the days and times she played. I believed she remembered what registered as important in her mind, and Bingo was important.

Dad loved men's club. Men's club consisted of eating donuts and watching movies-two of his favorite activities.

Dad's other passion was art class. Another thing I never had to remind him of. Dad's instructor was a retired art teacher. She selected a picture for her students to trace, and then they created their masterpieces using water colors. Dad with his one good eye labored for hours on his masterpieces. Everyone in our family had a cherished Leonard original hanging in their home.

BABY BOY (7/30/2010)

Today, we were blessed by the birth of our new grandson, Dante. The baby was delivered via c-section. I reminded Mom and Dad several times the baby would be delivered around one that afternoon. I promised to call them as soon as their new great-grandson arrived.

They had forgotten and attended their weekly movie. Years before, they would have been anxiously waiting by the phone for the good news.

I was finally able to reach them at three-thirty. They were overjoyed to hear the good news, and all the details about their great-grandson. When Mom heard Dante was born at one o'clock she scolded me, "Why did you wait so long to call?"

GOODBYE MOM (8/6/2010)

Mom and Dad came over for lunch. I hated to admit this, but at times I found it difficult having my parents over. I struggled to have a meaningful conversation. I was also having trouble accepting that tomorrow Mom might not remember anything about the day.

We "Skyped" my daughter and introduced our grandson to his great-grandparents. They were thrilled to see the baby. Several times Dad put his finger up to the computer screen, thinking he could touch the baby.

Mom was getting worse and starting to repeat herself again. I was learning to accept that my mother was gradually disappearing from my life.

After we drove them home, I called my cousin, who for years was her parents' caregiver. For my sanity I needed to share my experiences and feelings. I told her my parents had been over for dinner and admitted it was getting to be a challenge to have them at my house or even to take them out.

She understood completely. She confided to having had similar feelings with her parents, and warned me visiting my parents would become more difficult, too, especially when they stopped remembering I was there.

Damn, I hated seeing my parent deteriorate.

When I called Mom later that evening, she didn't remember seeing her great-grandson.

Dad wanted to talk to me, and informed me that their toilet was broken. He said he notified the receptionist, and someone would be there to fix it soon. I invited them to spend the night, but they politely refused. I knew they would be more comfortable in their own place. Dad also explained that they were able to use the toilet down the hall.

In the background I could hear Mom. "It's not far to walk. We can manage nicely, and neither one of us gets up in the middle of the night."

I assumed the work order would be addressed soon. I should have been smarter and realized that everyone over the age of sixty got up and made a visit to the bathroom at least once a night.

PLEASE GIVE ME STRENGTH (8/8/2010)

Mom informed me this morning that her watch was missing, so I decided to visit my parents and search for the watch. When I arrived, they were in the dining room finishing lunch. Before I entered, the activities director pulled me aside.

"Has anyone contacted you regarding your father?" She asked.

"No." I could not image what he had done. Maybe he was found taking toilet paper from the restroom.

"The security guard saw him the other day wandering in the hall around one-thirty in the morning wearing only his T-shirt and Depends."

Relief came upon me as I replied, "His toilet was broken, and the maintenance man had instructed him to use the one down the hall. The toilet was fixed yesterday."

Walking away, I started to laugh, picturing Dad half asleep pushing his walker down the hall, clad in a T-shirt and Depends, unconcerned about being seen. All I could envision was a cross between old Father Time and the New Year's Baby.

I walked with my parents back to their apartment after lunch. A strange smell permeated the kitchen. Several minutes passed before I determined where it was coming from and what it was. I'm not sure I could figure out what happened or how it happened, but I knew the odor was poop.

The trash can was soiled inside and outside with traces of feces. My guess was someone did not make it down the hall in time. How neither one could smell it was beyond me, until I remembered reading that losing your sense of smell might be a sign of Alzheimer's.

I disinfected and washed the trash can in the shower and cleaned their kitchen floor and bathroom.

Mom kept asking me what I was doing. "I'm cleaning," I said.

"Oh, leave it for the cleaning lady. That's what she gets paid to do."

In my mind, I replied, *"She doesn't get paid to do this shitty job."*

To make matters worse, I had asked Mom to sign a birthday card to send to my daughter. She signed the card, and then asked me at least five times in a matter of minutes, "Who is the card was for?"

My feelings at that point were difficult to describe. I was emotionally drained knowing that my parents were clueless. Inside, I kept asking God for strength and forgiveness because I didn't know these people, and at times like that I was finding it difficult to love them. Up until now I assumed I had a good handle on caregiving, and I was in control of everything. I fooled myself into believing this.

I gave them each a kiss good-bye. Mom's parting comment was, "We love you." Hearing her words brought a smile back to my face.

Finding the watch would have to wait for another day.

TOILET PAPER (8/11/2010)

Jim went to his weekly Wednesday morning men's church group, and we planned to meet afterward. I gave Mom and Dad a call. While on the phone she shouted, "What do you want, Len? Sit there and wait a few minutes." She came back on the phone. "Your Dad's on the toilet and can't find any toilet paper."

"Mom, it's in the front-hall closet. I'll hang up, and you can go get it for him."

"Oh, he can sit there for a minute until we get off the phone."

"I think you should get it for him now," I stated.

"All right, I'll go get it for him." She hung up the phone.

An hour later I met Jim. First thing out of his mouth was, "I got a panic call from your Dad. He said they have no toilet paper."

I was certain they had plenty, but we stopped to buy some and went to drop it off.

Dad was thrilled when he saw the toilet paper. I opened the front hall closet, and there in plain sight was a package of toilet paper containing nine rolls.

"Len, why didn't you look in the closet?" Mom asked.

I FORGET (8/12/2010)

Frequently Mom came out with some astute statements. She reminded me often, "I forget everything these days."

My reply was always the same. "At least you admit it to yourself. Some people don't acknowledge their memory loss."

"Well they're not fooling anyone but themselves, and probably not fooling themselves, either," she replied with a serious expression on her face.

EYE SEE YOU (8/20/2010)

Dad had an appointment with his ophthalmologist. Mom, Dad, and I marched into the office. We waited the usual forty-five minutes before getting called into the examination room. I left Mom with a magazine and led Dad into the room.

Fortunately, Dad's bad eye had not changed, but he did have a cataract in the good eye. The doctor indicated cataract surgery might improve his vision, but left the decision up to us.

When we left I explained everything to Dad and asked what he would like to do.

After several minutes he replied,

"No operation. Not at my age. Why bother?"

SURPRISE (8/23/2010)

Lenny called last week and said he was thinking of surprising Mom and Dad with a short weekend visit. He had started a new job, so weekends were the best time for him to travel. He had taken early retirement from an airline and had flight benefits. The only restriction was he had to fly standby and was never sure about seat availability until the last minute. The only flights available had him arriving

Saturday afternoon, and leaving early Sunday. The visit would be very short, but I was happy he planned to come.

I warned him not to get disappointed if Mom didn't remember his visit.

Jim and I picked my brother up at the airport and drove him to my parents' apartment. When we got to the parking lot outside their building, my brother phoned them. Mom answered the phone. He asked her to go outside onto their porch to check if it was raining. We were standing right below her porch balcony. After much convincing, she finally went to the door, opened it, and walked out. We were waving, and she waved back. Then she shouted, "Oh, my God, it's Lenny!"

We told her we would meet her upstairs. As we got off the elevator, there she was, without her walker, wobbling very quickly down the hall. She never let Dad know my brother was there. Trailing behind her, Dad was equally thrilled when he saw his son, and understood why his wife had charged out of their apartment.

We had a great afternoon and evening with my brother. Mom and Dad were so happy that he had come to visit.

I was astonished that Mom asked the next morning if my brother got off on time. I was so pleased that she remembered. But as expected, the memory was short lived. Later in the day she didn't remember the visit. When reminded she replied, "Oh yeah, it was so good to see your brother."

I knew it was my actress-mother responding.

HAPPY BIRTHDAY (9/8/2010)

First thing this morning, I called Mom to wish her a happy eighty-seventh birthday, and to remind her we would be going out to dinner to celebrate.

She answered the phone quicker than usual, and she was delighted to hear me singing *Happy Birthday*.

"Is today really my birthday?"

"Yes it is," I answered.

"Well, then it is quite appropriate that I am standing here talking to you in my birthday suit!"

THE TOILET (9/24/2010)

Armed with toilet paper, Kleenex, Depends, and two new blouses for Mom, I ventured over to see my parents. A staff member at their community had told me that older people go through lots of paper products. Was she ever right!

When I had called earlier, they had informed me their new toilet overflowed. I called to check and the maintenance man informed me the toilet was fixed.

They greeted me with a big hello and as usual were happy to see me.

As I walked into the bedroom to put the Depends in the closet, I noticed the carpet leading into the bathroom marked with a brownish-yellow spot approximately two feet by two feet. A trail of walker wheel marks had also been made from the bathroom to the living room.

The toilet water must have flowed into their bedroom and the wet wheels on their walkers left the black trail on the carpet. Neither Mom nor Dad could remember if the water leaked into the bedroom. As I tried to clean the spot, Mom kept telling me that I didn't need to clean the carpet.

"The cleaning person will do that," she announced.

I did my best, but the stain wouldn't disappear. My patience was hanging by a thin thread, and the thread was unraveling quickly every time my mother denied that the spot was a result of the over-flowing toilet.

I noticed another large brownish-yellow spot on the living room carpet bordering the kitchen. I was perplexed. Again neither one of them could tell me what happened. The only thing I could conjure up in my mind was that they tried wiping up the bathroom floor and put the wet paper towels in the kitchen trash can. Somehow the trash can tipped over and the liquid ran onto the living room carpet.

Cleaning the second spot wouldn't have been so bad if my mother wasn't constantly repeating, "What are you doing? You don't need to clean the carpet."

When asked what happened, she offered the same reply. "Oh, that spot has always been there."

It amazed me that neither one of them was concerned with the dirty carpet or remembered what had happened.

Dad shared he had gone down the hall to the bathroom but when I asked if Mom did the same, "Don't know," was his reply. Finally, after asking the question several times, Mom answered.

"I could not wait to go all the way down the hall, so you do what you have to do. I peed in the trash can."

A year ago, I would never have believed what I was hearing, but these days nothing surprised me.

When I got home I asked Jim to pour me a scotch. The visit had drained me.

WEIGHT WATCHERS (9/27/2010)

I took Mom and Dad to the doctor for their six-month routine checkup. Mom approached the scale as if it were shark-infested waters, one toe at a time. As the nurse began to move the weights farther and farther to the right, Mom's protests increased in volume.

"I need to take off my shoes! The scale is wrong! Don't forget to subtract for my clothes!"

The nurse left. I should have kept my thoughts to myself, but I could not.

"Mom, you have gained two pounds a month for the last year. You need to do more walking."

"I'm not fat. It's my big boobs."

After reviewing their blood test results and examining my parents, the doctor turned to me and said: "You and I should be in such good health."

He looked at Mom and Dad. "Walk. You both need to walk more."

When Mom and Dad first moved to Savannah, they walked almost every day, and then gradually stopped. The grounds around their building were beautiful and provided numerous places to walk.

Dad didn't answer the doctor, but Mom replied to his advice. "We walk all the time. We walk to breakfast, lunch, and dinner."

HAPPY 61st WEDDING ANNIVERSARY (9/28/2010)

Jim and I decided to have dinner with Mom and Dad at their retirement residence to celebrate their anniversary.

We bought a bottle of champagne to mark the occasion. A larger table was set up so their usual dining friends could join in our celebration.

Trying to keep the conversation going, I asked Dad what he remembered about his wedding day.

He thought and thought and then turned to look at my mother. He replied with a mischievous smirk. "I remember your mother asking if it would ever end."

At first I didn't understand the "it" he was referring to. So I continued to question him.

"What would end? The wedding reception?"

He smiled broadly and replied. "No, you know when was *I* going to stop," he said, still smiling.

Now I heard more than any child wanted to hear. We all smiled, somewhat embarrassed, and ate the rest of our dinner in silence. Jim filled my glass with more champagne.

HAPPY BIRTHDAY, JIM (10/2/2010)

Growing up, birthdays were a special day and celebrated with gifts, the person's favorite dinner, and cake. For Jim's birthday, I continued to be the planner, ensuring the day was memorable and fun.

I had planned to start the day with his favorite breakfast and end with our traditional steak dinner, accompanied by our favorite wine and cake.

I gave Jim several suggestions for things to do during the day. He wanted to go downtown to the Oktoberfest.

We had a great time, and driving home I decided to call Mom and Dad.

Dad answered the phone, and before I could ask how he was, I heard, "The toilet is broken again."

Jim felt we would have a better dinner if we went to check out the toilet. He was probably right.

The maintenance man had already stopped by to unplug the problem by the time we arrived.

I was not sure why anyone would install a low-water flush toilet in a senior home. Trying to explain to two octogenarians why they needed to hold the handle down longer to make sure the toilet bowl filled with water was impossible. I tried and failed.

Jim decided he would give it a try. He patiently showed Dad how to hold the handle down. After watching Dad flush the toilet at least ten times, Jim felt Dad was ready to train his wife.

The maintenance man called me the next day. He informed me he was going to replace the toilet with a high-impact flushing toilet.

"Yeah," I thought to myself.

I wondered how many times my Dad called him to complain before the maintenance man decided to switch toilets.

MARRIAGE (10/4/2010)

It had been two and a half years since we took the farewell pictures in front of my parents' old home and brought the two of them to Savannah. Jim and I agreed - and still do - that it would be better for all of us to have my parents close. Neither of us imagined or understood the amount of time and effort required to be a caregiver, or the affect it could have on our marriage.

Jim had been wonderful. Not once had he expressed any frustration when we had to rush over to fix their toilet or to take one of them to the emergency room. He never said no when I wanted to have my parents over for a meal or take them out to lunch. He had been nothing but patient, but caring for my parents was more work than either one of us had anticipated.

My parents had also been great, and even though Mom forgot things, she always remembered to tell me to go home to Jim and not waste my time with them.

In some respects our marriage has gotten stronger, and we have developed a deeper respect for each other. We try to stay positive and keep a sense of humor. Jim and I know our marriage is strong and will survive these challenges. I just hope I will survive.

UROLOGIST (10/6/2010)

Who said you can't teach an old dog new tricks? Today was Dad's routine checkup with the urologist. This time I called in advance to get permission to have Dad collect his urine specimen at home. The doctor's nurse granted permission, and I picked up the plastic cup. Dad successfully peed into the container that I placed in a small brown paper bag. I thought it was humorous that the bag came from the Jockey store and was stamped *Jockey* on the front.

I asked Mom if she wanted to come for the ride.

"You have enough on your hands. You don't need me," she replied.

As Dad and I were walking out the door, Mom was right behind us. I knew she didn't want to stay home alone.

Dad received a clean bill of health from the doctor, and instructed to see him again in about six months or if there was a problem. Dad had blood in his urine, which had shown up on his last couple of tests, but because Dad was almost ninety, the doctor was not concerned.

To celebrate one less doctor's visit, I took Mom and Dad to Chick-fil-A and then to McDonald's for an ice cream. I didn't feel guilty buying the ice cream because Mom was in the habit of ordering it at every meal. Dad loved his chicken sandwich and Mom never said no to an ice cream cone.

When we got back to their building, the residents were finishing lunch. Mom asked what was going on in the dining room. I explained they were finishing up lunch.

"Good, let's go sit and have some ice cream for dessert," she chimed.

"You had ice cream. You need to go for a walk."

Proceeding out the door, I encouraged them to walk me to my car and then to go for a short stroll. They trailed a few yards behind, and I heard Mom talking to Dad.

"Let's wait until she leaves and then we can go upstairs."

I turned around. "I can hear you and that's cheating."

With a red face she whispered, "Len, we got caught."

SWOLLEN TOE (10/23/2010)

Today was one of those glorious days that made me happy to be alive. The sky was crystal blue, a light fall breeze filled the fresh, crisp, autumn air, and the temperature was a pleasant seventy-nine degrees. I was feeling great as I drove the eight miles to Mom and Dad's apartment. I hadn't seen them in almost a week and I was eager to see them. Jim and I needed a break and had taken our sailboat out for a few days. The cruise rejuvenated us.

I called yesterday and asked my mother if they had been walking.

"Not really," she answered.

"Why not?"

"My big toe hurts. It's swollen."

Jim wanted to rush over to check, but I felt it could wait since she didn't express a great deal of pain.

Now I knocked on their door. Mom greeted me with, "Come on in. It's open."

My excitement fizzled as I walked in to the smell of, as I call it, "old" age. The apartment smelled of stale air mixed with urine. The blinds, lights, and windows were all tightly closed. It was noon, and I must have awakened both of them. They usually had breakfast late in the morning between nine and ten, so by eleven they were ready for the first nap of the day. I'm convinced both my parents had lost their sense of smell. I opened all the blinds, the patio door, and bedroom windows.

I pulled a Clorox wipe from their bathroom and cleaned the yellow streak of urine that dripped down the front of the toilet and onto the floor. Dad didn't quite hit the mark these days. Cleaning put me back in a better mood. The smell of fresh air and "Clorox clean" seemed to help.

I asked Mom how her toe felt and led her to the bedroom, so I could take a better look. As with the time before, I neither saw nor felt anything unusual.

"Mom, your toe looks fine to me. Where does it hurt?"

With a guilty look and grin she answered, "Well, I lied. My toe is fine."

My immediate reply was, "What?"

"Well, I don't feel like walking, so I lied."

"Mom, you can't do that. Didn't you teach me never to lie?"

She did not hesitate to answer. "I did. But I'm old, so it's okay."

WORRY ABOUT YOURSELF (10/30/2010)

One day I was telling my four-year-old granddaughter Isabella to finish her dinner. She looked at me with a most serious expression and said, "Worry about yourself, Grandma."

I should take her advice. I worried about everyone but me.

GEORGIA PECANS (11/19/2010)

Jim and I thought it would be fun to take Mom and Dad for a ride to the farmer's market for pecans.

Dad answered the phone this morning when I called to ask if they would like to come for the ride. He replied without hesitation. "No, we have too much laundry to do. We don't have any clean clothes."

I could not believe they had run out of clean clothes.

"Dad, please put Mom on the phone."

"Hi, dear, how are you?" she said.

"Would you and Pop like to go for a ride to get pecans."

"Oh, that sounds so nice. Let me ask your Dad."

I heard her ask him, and he quickly answered, "Great."

I was learning that sometimes it took two tries to get a good answer.

They were waiting outside when we arrived.

Mom managed to entertain us by pointing out every yellow car she saw. It had been two and a half years, and her fascination for yellow cars had not diminished. I could count on her to find every yellow car on the road, and she announced each and every time one passed that she didn't like yellow cars.

Mom and Dad enjoyed the ride and the sampling of the pecans and sugar cane. Jim decided having an ice cream cone for lunch would be a great idea and Mom needed no encouragement to agree.

That night I called Mom, and told her Jim and I had fun with them today. She remembered nothing about the day – not the drive, eating fresh pecans, drinking sugar cane or the ice cream lunch. When she asked me what we had done, I heard Dad in the background shouting: "Pecans and ice cream."

"Sometimes he gets mad at me for not remembering. I can't help it. I can't remember anything anymore, and I hate it. Sometimes, I want to kill myself," she told me.

I tried to recall events for her and made sure I emphasized how much she had enjoyed what we did. She was happy to have me review the day's activities even though she had forgotten them. She thanked me for helping her remember.

Once again I was convinced that keeping Mom on the Citalopram to avoid depression was a good idea. I was worried at first she might get addicted to the medication. When I discussed this with Jim, he looked at me puzzled and stated. "She's eighty-seven, what difference does it make?"

FOOT BONE CONNECTED TO THE LEG BONE
(11/23/2010)

Mom still was complaining about her toe, so I made an appointment with the podiatrist.

He recognized Mom and welcomed her back. She stared at the doctor and said, "I think I've been here before. You look familiar."

The doctor said her nail was pressing into the toe and causing pain. She winced every time the doctor touched her toe, but felt better when he was done cutting her toenails.

My car was in for service. Jim dropped us off and went to Home Depot. Waiting for him to pick us up, Mom asked nine times, "What are we doing here?"

Then she answered her own question, "The foot doctor. Am I right? Have I seen him yet?"

This was the week of doctor appointments.

Mom had a bone-density test scheduled the next day, so as she was getting out of the car I reminded her. With a confused expression, she said, "Why are you wasting your time and my money on a bone-density test? My bones are old, and the test will only tell you that I have old bones, and old bones have problems."

I called the following morning at eight-thirty. Mom was still in bed. I reminded her that she needed to get ready, and I would be there to pick her up shortly.

"Where are we going today?" she asked.

I knew she would forget. I heard Dad in the background. "You're going to the doctor's office."

Mom's reply, "They stole my watch, so I don't know what time it is." I could hear her take a deep breath. "I have this letter, and I want you to read it. Hold on, let me get it."

"Mom, no. I'll look at it later. Get up, wash, and have breakfast. I'll be there shortly."

I decided to go over early to do some housework and make sure she was ready on time. Mom did no housework, and the weekly cleaning people were not allowed by management to touch any personal items. They vacuumed, cleaned the bathroom, washed the kitchen floor and cleaned the kitchen counter tops. I tried to dust the furniture every week.

When I arrived, my parents were walking out the door to go have breakfast. Mom had already forgotten she was going for a bone density test. I noticed Dad's pants were zipped halfway. Every time I saw him, he was wearing a sweater, so I never noticed how tight his pants were around the waist. I had asked him a million times if he needed larger pants, and his reply was a quick and firm no.

While they were having breakfast, I cleaned.

As I approached their bedroom, the now-familiar and foul smell of urine filled my nostrils. On the floor of the closet were two stained pants. I was not sure what came over me, but my eyes filled with tears. This was not the job I signed up for; these were not the people I loved. I wanted to be the child, not the parent. I wanted the mother who listened without judgment and was there with good advice. I wanted the father who was strong and could fix anything. These people had stopped caring and were tired of life.

In the middle of my pity party, I was startled by the nurse who helped Dad shower. She was standing behind me. Mom and Dad never locked their door anymore. She was walking by and decided to check in on them.

I restrained myself from rushing into her arms for a pity hug. I asked if she was aware that Dad was wetting his pants and if it was time to move them to assisted living. She explained he was not comfortable sleeping in his bed and had spent the last few nights sleeping in his living room chair. He preferred to sleep with his head elevated. My dad never complained about anything. She added that this was not unusual for the elderly. Needless to say I was surprised, but I guessed nothing should have surprised me anymore.

She explained that he was waiting too long before going to the bathroom and sometimes missed the bowl. She also assured me they were doing fine and not yet ready for assisted living.

I dusted the furniture, put away the clean laundry, and rinsed out Dad's pants. Once again I found the stolen watch "they" had taken.

By the time Mom and Dad had returned from breakfast, I was drained of energy. I decided to take Mom's advice and canceled her test. Even if she has bone deterioration, what could be done for an eighty-seven-year-old? I felt she didn't need another pill.

UGLY SHOES (11/30/2010)

The podiatrist recommended I get Mom some larger shoes - something like tennis shoes, which would provide her with more support and would be roomier than her current shoes. She liked to wear slip-on shoes.

I saw Dr. Scholl's shoes being advertised in one of the Sunday magazines and ordered two pairs, navy and black. They looked comfortable, with Velcro straps rather than laces, and somewhat stylish. I thought the Velcro straps would be easier than tying shoelaces. I was excited to show Mom.

I hadn't even gotten the shoes out of the box when Mom shouted, "I'm not wearing those shoes! They are ugly shoes that old ladies wear."

Mom and Dad grew up in an ethnic neighborhood, with Italian, Irish, Polish, and German neighbors. The shoes reminded her of the ones all the Polish mothers would wear. They were sturdy and would last a lifetime.

As with everything I buy them now, I "lied" about the price. It was so long since Mom and Dad had shopped that they lost all understanding of current prices, the economy, and the cost of living. I shopped for them. They never saw a bill, and were living in the past regarding the value of a dollar. They still wanted to know what items cost since, as mom puts it, "it's our money." I decided from now on it was easier to give them a price they felt was a "good deal" than give them the actual cost. I determined they would not flinch at anything priced under ten dollars. This made it easier and put less stress on Mom.

When I explained the shoes were so cheap they could not be returned, she finally agreed to keep them.

34-24-34 (12/1/2010)

The days were getting colder, and Mom could no longer fit into the coat I bought her last year.

Today, I went shopping for a new coat. Mom wore a petite because of her height which made the task more challenging. I went to five stores before I found a coat that might fit her and three heavy sweaters. The coat was a size 3X, and the sweaters were size 2X. I drove over to have Mom try them on.

The coat did not fit. Only one of the sweaters fit, and to make matters worse she only liked to wear blue clothing. The sweater was black and she made it clear, it was not her favorite color. She proceeded to say, "I'll never wear it."

I drove back to the store and purchased the other two sweaters in the largest size sold, and I was lucky one came in blue.

Last year's coat would have to do, even if it no longer zipped up. Fortunately, the temperature never got too cold in Savannah.

CHURCH MUSIC (12/5/2010)

On the first Saturday of the month, our church had an early evening service accompanied by the Screaming Hamsters guitar group. The group's name was descriptive enough to convey that the service was very upbeat with praise music. We had taken Mom and Dad a few times after they moved to Savannah.

Dad asked every time we saw him, "Does your church still have that service with music?"

One night, we decided to take my parents with us. Dad loved the service. Several times I noticed his feet tapping to the beat of the music, and he even attempted to sing *Amazing Grace* – off key.

After church, we went to the local barbecue restaurant for dinner.

My parents thanked us all the way home for such a good time.

When we returned to their place, the last of the dinner residents were leaving the dining room. Mom immediately asked, "Should we go for dinner now?"

She didn't remember having just eaten, nor did her mind tell her she was full.

FEELING OKAY (12/11/2010)

I called today, and Dad answered the phone. He sounded awful. He was all congested. Yesterday, I asked him if he was feeling sick, and he said he felt okay.

I contacted the pharmacist to see if he could take any cold pills with his usual medications. The pharmacist explained plain Claritin should be fine. Jim and I dropped everything to go to the pharmacy and bought Dad the pills.

Dad looked as bad as he sounded. Since it was Saturday, I could not take him to the doctor, and so we would have to go to the emergency room. The day was cold and rainy. He appeared visibly melancholy and tired. I hated to think of dragging him out on such a miserable day. I asked him if he felt bad enough to go to the emergency room. He shouted, "No!" I gave him a pill and said a prayer that he would feel better.

We offered to get him some chicken soup from his favorite fast food restaurant. He answered with another emphatic no. When asked again two minutes later, he said, "That would be nice."

Off we went for the soup. Once back in their apartment, I set it out on the table and helped Dad into the kitchen. He sat down and took two small spoonfuls.

Struggling for words, he said, "I'm not hungry."

With that, I insisted he go right to bed. He obeyed.

I requested dinner be delivered to their room, and when I called later he sounded much better.

I had difficulty knowing when my parents should be taken to the doctor or emergency room. I was not sure they even knew how they felt anymore.

I find I'm no longer compelled to rush them for treatment every time they express pain. I'm trying to do a better job at analyzing the need.

ONCE A MARINE ALWAYS A MARINE (12/13/2010)

Dad was still not feeling like himself. I called the doctor's office to get an appointment. Thanks to their doctor's attentive nurse, she made an appointment for him to be examined that morning.

I led Dad to a seat in the waiting room, signed him in, and then sat beside him. Shortly after, we were called into the examination room. We were only in the room for a few seconds when Dad shouted.

"My hat! Where's my hat?"

I retraced our steps back to the car, the waiting room, and the path we took to the examination room. No hat. I knew he had it with him because I put it on his head an hour before. I remembered he had it walking into the waiting area.

He was very upset, and so was I. Who would take a hat that belonged to a World War II veteran? I left my name at the front desk in case someone found it, and then retraced our steps twice. Still, no hat.

The doctor examined Dad and determined he had bronchitis.

As we left, I checked again at the front desk. No one had found a hat.

Dad was very quiet on the way home. He finally spoke up.

"Would you get me another cap?"

This was the first time in my life my father had asked me for anything other than paper products and Coke. He was a resilient man.

MY CAP (12/17/2010)

I called to remind Dad to take his pills. Mom answered the phone. I asked her how he felt.

"He feels with his hands like everyone else. How do I know how he feels? You need to ask him." I was not sure whether Mom was attempting to be funny or sarcastic.

When Dad got on the phone, the first words out of his mouth were, "Did you find my cap?"

He had been asking me the same question for four days now. I went online and even called the Parris Island Marine gift shop. I determined WWII veterans were not a marketable audience.

I found only one website that carried a World War II veteran's cap. I ordered him a new one, but I kept thinking how sad it was that someone would take a cap belonging to an eighty-nine-year-old man.

FIELD TRIP (12/21/10)

We were going to Marisa and Ricardo's house for Christmas. I decided to get Mom and Dad packed a couple of days early. Next time, I will know better than to do it while they were around.

Mom insisted she could pack for herself. Every time I put something in the suitcase she would take it out. Because I learned to foster a good attitude, I found her helping humorous. Otherwise I might have gone nuts. I finally allowed Mom to pick out what she wanted to wear.

After what felt like hours, the suitcases were packed. I kept hoping the clothes would still be in the suitcase when Jim and I came back to pick them up.

MERRY CHRISTMAS (12/23/2010)

After Mom and Dad had taken showers and Mom got her hair washed and set, the "sleigh" heading to Charleston left Savannah. Neither Mom nor Dad recalled me packing their suitcases two days before.

To distract Mom from asking for the hundredth time if I had written everyone a check for Christmas, I decided to play count the yellow cars/trucks. Naturally, Mom won. It was a great way to pass the two and a half hour car ride.

We made a rest stop halfway. As a precaution, I had them wear Depends. Mom made grunting sounds the whole time she was in the restroom. I asked if she needed help and she replied, "I'm doing fine."

Jim and Dad were already outside when we got to the car. Jim was grinning and proceeded to tell me that when he turned from the urinal, there Dad was, standing with the stall door wide open and his pants and Depends around his knees, peeing. Jim held the stall door closed until Dad had finished.

Fortunately, the rest of the ride was uneventful.

We had a wonderful Christmas celebration. Mom and Dad were so happy to see their great-grandchildren. Dad pushed his walker aside to dance to the beat of Christmas songs with his granddaughter.

On the first morning of our visit, they woke up confused, forgetting where they were. Mom asked if they were at Teresa's house. Teresa was a neighbor and good friend from their old neighborhood. They had never slept at Teresa's house.

During Christmas Eve dinner, out of the blue Dad asked, "Do you remember when Connie - another neighbor from their old street - got robbed?"

I did remember and this happened at least thirty years before.

Mom seemed startled and started to laugh. "Besides nothing, what does that have to do with the conversation at hand?" Her mind was going but her wit remained intact.

ARE YOU THERE (12/29/2010)

I went over to my parents' apartment to collect some clothes Mom had grown out of for our church thrift store. I also wanted to dust and do a few other chores before my brother and his family came to visit. They were driving down from New Jersey to spend New Year's Eve with us.

When I arrived, Mom sounded surprised to hear my brother was coming to visit, even though she and I had talked about this all month. She asked me if Christmas had passed which confirmed my belief that she remembered very little about our wonderful holiday. I explained Christmas had been the week before, and I reminded her of how we spent the holiday.

"Oh. Yeah. You know it's awful not to remember anything," she said.

Her concern about remembering had become a recurring conversation. It must be terrible not to remember. I was feeling so sad for my mother.

Dad kept dozing off as I dusted around him. Mom kept repeating the same sentence. "You don't have to dust. I'm capable of doing that."

I thought, *"Yes, Mom, you are. But you don't do it."*

At one point Dad woke up and blurted out, "I need to get those pictures developed." He must have been dreaming.

Mom gave him a puzzled look. "Len, you're out of it. What are you talking about?"

"I don't know," was his answer.

She turned toward me. "You know, sometimes I worry about your Dad. He's not always there."

Again I thought, *"I worry about both of you. Sometimes neither one of you is there."*

NEW YEAR'S EVE (12/31/2010)

Lenny, Marie and Michael came to visit after Christmas. My brother, sister-in-law, nephew, and Jim and I joined my parents for their New Year's Eve dinner dance.

We got to my parents' apartment early enough to help them get dressed for the party.

Dad sprang to his feet when we informed him there would be dancing. He went into the bedroom to put on his gray slacks and navy blazer. Mom, on the other hand, kept questioning why she needed to change out of her multi-food-stained top.

My sister-in-law tried to coax Mom into changing her clothes. Mom was not budging. Finally in a voice that a mother would use with her children, I said, "Mom, get up now, and I'll help you change your clothes. If you don't change, you can't go to the party."

She immediately scampered into the bedroom.

We had a wonderful evening, and the night ended singing *Auld Lang Syne* and wishing each other Happy New Year. It was seven-thirty in the evening.

CHAPTER 5
YEAR FOUR

DON'T LOSE IT (1/5/2011)

Dad's new cap arrived, and I anxiously went to deliver it. When I proclaimed I had his new cap, he got very excited.

"Can I see it?"

As I handed him the cap, his smile was the widest I had ever seen. He immediately put it on his head and said, "I love it."

Mom chimed in, "Now don't lose it."

She could remember Dad losing his cap, but could not remember my brother's visit. How sad was that?

OLD AGE (1/12/2011)

No one wants to get old. No one wants to see their body and mind deteriorate. No one wants to become dependent on their family or strangers but it will happen to each of us.

As one gets older, our actions are often compared to those of babies, but babies develop, learn, and get stronger every day. For the elderly, it was the opposite. They regress, show signs of memory loss, and become weaker every day.

I was not sure why I came to this revelation today except that I arrived at Mom and Dad's as they were doing chair aerobics. I estimated the average age of the people trying to kick their legs up, move their head from side to side, and raise their arms must have been eighty-five.

A smile came across my face as I watched Dad's legs come off the floor about an inch and Mom's about four inches. When it came to the side-to-side head moves, I had to watch very closely to see the slight movement left and right. Everyone was so serious attempting to move their bodies.

LIFE THROUGH CHEMISTRY (1/15/2011)

Jim and I picked Mom and Dad up for one of the pleasures they still loved to indulge in: a good breakfast of freshly ground coffee and homemade blueberry and Georgia pecan pancakes.

On the drive over to our house, I noticed Dad was more alert and talkative than usual, and Mom was in a very good mood.

We talked all during breakfast, and they were still more engaged than normal on the ride home. Mom kept thanking God for a wonderful day and then chimed in, "He must be getting tired of hearing from me."

I was pleased and puzzled by the improvement in their behavior.

While Jim was helping them get out of the SUV, I ran ahead to fill their pillboxes. It was then that I found my answer. Neither one of them had taken their nighttime pills for the last two days.

Had we become an overmedicated world?

90 YEARS (1/19/2011)

In a couple of days Dad would be ninety years old. I couldn't even imagine how he felt reaching this milestone. Is he happy or fearful because death had to be approaching very soon?

No matter how Dad felt about his birthday, he needed to celebrate. I put together an invitation that everyone in his independent living community received. Since Dad loved to dance, his party would include music. I hired a trio to play and ordered a large birthday cake. The party was to take place during their normal dinner.

Marisa, Ricardo, Isabella, Dante, and some good friends planned to join us for dinner to celebrate Dad's birthday.

I decided because he was ninety, it would be better to tell Dad about the party rather than shock his system with a surprise.

Dad rarely showed emotion. His genuine excitement over the party took me aback. He was telling everyone about the party. He invited his art teacher, the nurses who helped him shower, and who knew how many others to the celebration.

Every time I called, he would ask me what he should wear to the party. I decided to buy him a new pair of gray dress slacks, and I even took one of his shirts home to iron. Mom stopped ironing clothes years ago.

HAPPY 90th BIRTHDAY LEONARD (1/21/2011)

We arrived at Mom and Dad's a couple of hours before the party. They were both very happy to see their two great-grandchildren.

Dad excused himself and went into the bathroom. After twenty minutes, I stood by the bathroom door and called out. "Are you okay?"

"Yes."

Several more minutes passed before he came out of the bathroom. Small blotches of shaving cream revealed why he had been in the bathroom for so long. I helped him get dressed. He was very excited.

As we exited the elevator on the first floor, I was surprised by the large turnout of residents approaching Dad as he entered the dining room. Several welcomed him to the Nineties Club.

I wasn't sure how he felt when the entire dining room started singing *Happy Birthday* or when he blew the numbered 9 and 0 candles out on his cake. His expression didn't seem to change until the musicians started to play, and Miss E asked him to dance with her. Dad jumped up from his chair and practically ran to the dance floor. Miss E was a member of the staff. My parents loved her. She was a rare individual treating all the residents with love and respect.

Dad proceeded to put one hand on his waist and moved his hips from side to side with the beat of the music. The entire room broke out in laughter. His dance moves consisted of the swaying of his hips, and a little Elvis-like pelvic roll, followed by twirling his partner. Tonight he was happy and not fearful.

Dancing changed him. He was no longer an old man but a person filled with energy, movement in his legs, and a song on his lips. He sang out loud, "I love my wife, I love my wife" as he danced with Miss E. Mom stopped dancing years ago. She never liked to dance and only danced slow with Dad. I considered his little song an attempt to make Mom feel included. She never felt left out, and was always happy to see him dancing.

My daughter, granddaughter, two friends, and I each had a turn dancing with Dad and several other residents. It was a wonderful celebration.

COFFEE (2/6/2011)

Jim and I invited Mom and Dad for breakfast. I reminded them to be ready in the morning at ten, in the lobby. Because I was getting resourceful, I made sure they wrote down the day, time, and place. I instructed them to put the reminder somewhere they would see it, which was usually on the kitchen table. I also started to call them an hour before the pick-up time.

After several attempts with no answer, I called the front desk and asked if my parents were around. The receptionist answered and immediately replied to my question. "Oh, yes, they're sitting right here."

I left to go pick them up.

They were happy to see me, and I surmised they had been sitting waiting for me for over an hour.

I ran upstairs to get Dad a jacket and noticed a large stain on the bedroom rug. It looked like someone spilled a cup of coffee.

While driving home, I asked, "Who spilled the coffee?"

Dead silence.

"Come on, what happened?"

Mom was the first to reply. "It wasn't me."

After another long pause and another denial by Mom, Dad finally chimed in. "Mary, it was you. You spilled a cup of coffee."

"I am not responsible for anything I don't remember, and I don't remember spilling coffee, so there," was her reply.

Then she laughed and said, "I guess I'm not responsible for much these days because I don't remember too much."

CHICK-FIL-A (3/15/2011)

As usual I called this morning to see how Mom and Dad were doing. Mom answered the phone.

"Your father wants to ask you a question."

"Mariann, when you get a chance - and no rush - would you get me a Chick-fil-A sandwich?"

I was taken aback because other than his request for a new Marine cap and paper products, he didn't ask for things.

The next morning, I picked them up at eleven-fifteen for an early lunch at Chick-fil-A. Getting to the restaurant before the lunchtime crowds made it easier to maneuver them and their walkers through the parking lot and inside.

Dad had a big smile on his face and was genuinely delighted to be going out for lunch. As we walked into the restaurant, the hostess, a pretty woman with short salt-and-pepper hair, greeted them. She saw Dad's cap and thanked him for serving his country. Dad nodded and said with a slight grin, "You're welcome."

He devoured his sandwich. The ironic part was the day Dad called asking to go to Chick-fil-A was the ninetieth birthday of S. Truett Cathy, the founder of Chick-fil-A. He and Dad were born the same year.

I needed to run an errand at Target and decided to take Mom and Dad with me. On the way we passed McDonald's, so I went to the drive-up window and ordered a chocolate and strawberry sundae. This would keep my parents happy and entertained while I ran my errand. They were so excited - a Chick-fil-A sandwich and a McDonald's sundae! Who could ask for anything better?

When I got back to the car the only trace of the sundaes was a spot of chocolate sauce on Dad's shirt.

I tried to remind Mom that she would be getting back before lunch was over in the dining room, and I reminded her that she didn't need to go in, because they had already eaten. To that she replied, "We did?"

SEMPER FI (3/20/2011)

Mom had some good days and some bad days.

I picked them up to bring them to our house for an Italian dinner. On the ride over, Mom started the conversation. "You should know I am really forgetting everything. Thank God for your Dad. He is still sharp. If it wasn't for him, I would be very depressed."

"Mom," I said, "Are you enjoying yourself right now?"

"Oh, yes."

"Then you should live for the moments. You can remember this moment, and you're having fun right now."

"Good idea. I will live for the moments," she replied happily.

She asked three times during our fifteen-minute ride what day it was, and Dad so sweetly said each time, "Mary, it's Saturday."

Witnessing Mom's mind slowly deteriorate must have been hard on Dad. He was taking on more responsibility, and never expressed anything but love for her. I respected my Dad more now than ever.

Dad was and will forever be a Marine. He truly lived by the Marine motto "Semper Fi - Always faithful."

HOUSECOAT (4/6/2011)

During our conversation, Mom asked if I would mind buying her a new housecoat. She informed me that when she wore hers to go down the hall to get her morning coffee, it was difficult to button.

I threw a fit. "Mom, you shouldn't wear your housecoat in the hall if you can't button it."

"Well, it's not like I have anything that most of these old fogies haven't seen before."

After our conversation, I got online to try to find one that would fit. Luckily, I was able to order one and had it shipped immediately.

Mom received it the next day but was having a difficult time coping with my spending nineteen dollars and ninety-five cents on a new housecoat. Even when I explained it was discounted forty percent, she still wanted me to return it because I had spent too much. I wouldn't dare tell her how much I spent on shipping, to save the residents the treat of seen her parading around with her boobs exposed in the halls.

The only way around the dilemma was to go to their apartment, have her try it on, remove all tags, and hide her old housecoat.

I did, and she now loved the new housecoat.

NEW PANTS (4/8/2011)

Every day I asked my parents if they needed anything. Dad was usually good at letting me know when they needed Depends, toilet paper, paper towels, soap, etc.

I answered the phone, and my father said, "I need pants. Some of mine don't fit anymore."

I was pleased that he was getting more vocal and expressing his needs to me.

The next time I went by the mall, I stopped into JCPenney and picked up two pair of elastic-waist pants size thirty-eight. I drove over to their apartment and had him try the pants on before I hemmed them. He thanked me and said they fit fine.

A couple of days later I dropped off the two new pants for him.

Two days later when I called, Dad answered the phone and before even saying hello he began, "Those new pants don't fit. They're too tight."

I took a deep breath to calm myself. Since I hemmed the pants, I could not return them.

So back to JCPenney I went for size forty, then back to Mom and Dad's apartment for another fitting. This time I followed him into the bedroom when he tried the pants on. They fit.

Two days later I left him the hemmed pants.

Five days had passed since the first pairs of pants were bought. I called this morning and Dad answered the phone.

"I need new pants. The ones you bought are too small."

This time I had a fit.

Raising my voice I said, "What? You tried them on the other day, and they were fine."

After calming down, I went online and bought Dad new pants, size forty-two with a full elastic waist and pre-hemmed.

They were more expensive but my sanity was worth the cost.

HAPPY EASTER (4/24/2011)

I wrestled with my conscience for weeks about being away from my parents at Easter. Our grandchildren from Connecticut, Katie and TJ, were coming to Charleston over spring break. They were leaving to go back home the Friday before Easter.

Since we were already in Charleston the week before Easter, it made sense we spend Easter there with Marisa and her family.

I brought my parents a hydrangea and each a very small chocolate bunny before we left. I knew Mom didn't need the candy, but after all, it was Easter and she would have been disappointed without it. I called a few times to make sure they had signed up for Easter Sunday brunch.

I talked to Mom several times today but didn't tell her we were in Charleston with her granddaughter and family. I didn't want her to feel bad. Mom never remembered it was Easter and sounded content. All my worrying was for nothing. Neither one of them was fazed by our not being together.

HAPPY 60th Birthday (5/3/2011)

Today was my sixtieth birthday. Growing older had never bothered me, but for some reason turning sixty made me feel uncomfortable.

I called Mom and Dad this morning. Mom answered with her usual, "Hello, how are you?" I proceeded to ask her if she knew what today was, and after much hesitation she answered, "It's May third."

I was certain I heard the rustling of the newspaper in the background, which she often referred to for the day and date. I reminded her yesterday that today was my birthday.

After several minutes she asked, "Is today your birthday?"

"Yes, Mom, it is."

"Oh, sorry I didn't remember. Happy birthday."

I couldn't begin to explain the emptiness I had. For the first time in sixty years my mother had forgotten my birthday. Dad never even got on the phone to wish me happy birthday.

Thanks to my husband, I had a fun and wonderful day.

Later in the day Marisa phoned to ask if Mom and Dad had wished me happy birthday. She had called in the morning to remind them. I explained that Mom had remembered after I more or less prompted her. My daughter shared that when she called earlier, my mother was very upset that she had forgotten. She shared Mom's words with me: "Imagine forgetting your own child's birthday. I made your mom, and I forgot the day. Isn't that terrible?"

As I did every night, I called my parents. They never mentioned my birthday. It was okay. I loved them and understood they really didn't want to forget but it still hurt. The funny part was soon they won't remember their own birthdays.

CONFESSION (5/25/2011)

"It's almost a relief when they reach the next step and are unable to go out." A friend who lost her mother several months ago said these words to me. She was a very good daughter and spent many years and considerable time caring for her mother who died in her nineties.

My friend explained that a point came when it was more difficult to take her mother out, and it became easier to go visit her. That point occurred when her mother fell and had to use a wheel chair.

A few months ago I would have been shocked by this comment and would never have believed I would understand. I must confess sometimes the stress gets to me, and I am beginning to understand.

REMOTE CONTROL (5/26/2011)

More than a week ago, Dad informed me the TV remote control wasn't working.

I had caught a stomach virus which kept me home and prevented me from seeing my parents until today.

I remembered they needed batteries for the remote control and drove to their apartment. When I arrived at their place the TV was off. I pressed the Power button on the remote, and the TV turned on to the Guide channel. But when I changed the channels, no matter what station I selected, all that appeared on the screen was snow.

I called downstairs to see if the building was having cable problems. The receptionist reminded me that I needed to use the Comcast remote control. Understanding that two remotes would confuse them, I had put the old one in a dresser draw. Somehow one of them found it. Nothing was wrong with the remote; they were using the wrong remote.

Then it dawned on me that for ten days Mom and Dad had only been watching the TV Guide channel.

It was times like this that my parents believed they created a genius.

TODAY (5/29/2011)

On Memorial Day weekend, Jim came up with a great idea. We would have Mom and Dad over for Sunday brunch, but cook and eat it on our dock. We were blessed to live on a river. My parents enjoyed sitting on our porch looking at the water but never went down to the dock. The dock was 150 feet from the house.

We carried out our coffee pot, waffle grill, plates, and everything else needed for brunch. Mom and Dad were thrilled as they pushed their walkers toward the dock. They stopped to rest once along the way to take in the fresh air and beautiful view.

I really think it was the first time Dad could see with clarity the boats passing by. Every time a boat motored or sailed by, he would point it out to us.

Mom repeated over and over, "This is wonderful."

We sat on the dock for hours. It was a fantastic day.

Driving home, Dad said, "Thank you for a great day."

"Len, what did we do today?" my mother asked.

9th HOLE (5/31/2011)

Judging from the way my golf game started this morning, I would have guessed the day would not go down as one of my best. Jim and I enjoyed walking nine holes of golf at our local military golf course. The course was open to the public, and inexpensive. It was the perfect course for golfers like us who were out to enjoy the exercise and occasionally played a good hole or two. It was located directly across the street from my parents' retirement community.

As I was teeing off on the last hole, my phone rang. I glimpsed at the phone's display and noticed it was my daughter. Marisa was at work and knew we planned to play golf this morning, so her call had to be important.

"Mom, I talked to Gram. She sounded fine, but told me she was sitting on the living-room floor. She didn't remember what happened and was getting up. I called the front desk and asked them to check on her."

We immediately stopped playing and drove over to Mom and Dad's apartment.

My game was a little off that day, and in an effort to lessen the tension, Jim and I laughed, saying that Mom planned the interruption.

When we got there she appeared to be in no pain and was smiling as usual, but still sitting on the floor. I estimated she had been there for two hours. Why my father never called us was beyond me.

Since we knew it was against the rules for staff to help lift independent residents, Jim and I were about to attempt to lift Mom. We had left the door to their apartment open as we rushed in. At that moment a staff member walked in, and bending the rules, assisted in getting Mom into her chair. We were grateful.

"What happened? Why was I on the floor?" Mom asked the questions, we were all hoping she would answer.

We helped her up from the chair and asked her to walk into the kitchen, so we could assess if she had hurt anything. She moved forward about six feet and said, "Ouch! That hurts." She was unable to put pressure on her left foot.

That meant another trip to the emergency room. I believed it would be best for Dad to stay behind.

The emergency medical technicians were called. Again, the EMTs were wonderful as they checked Mom and lifted her onto a stretcher for transport to the hospital. I could see her anxiety when the technicians began to strap her onto the stretcher.

"Why are you doing that? Are you afraid I'll run off?" Then she laughed.

During the fifteen-minute drive to the hospital, Mom continued to ask where I was. I had taken my usual seat next to the driver. I heard her and answered, "I'm here, Mom."

We spent two and a half hours in the emergency room getting Mom thoroughly checked out. The staff had performed blood work, took CT scans of every part of her body that moved, and X-rayed her ankle.

Fortunately the X-ray technician came out to double-check with me after my mother had told him the right ankle. Mom had a problem with "left" and "right" distinctions.

At that instant, the realization that a caregiver needed to be on top of everything came to me when I learned he was preparing to X-ray the wrong ankle.

The next step was to wait for the results, with Mom asking me over and over, "Why are we here?"

If someone had divulged to me that I would see both my parents' private parts, I would have cringed and immediately said, "No way." I've learned that a person should never say never.

Mom turned to me and proclaimed, "I have to pee."

I immediately went to get a nurse, who insisted we put Mom on a bedpan rather than get her up and help her to the bathroom. The nurse had informed me that she only recently started working in the hospital. Before I knew it, the nurse quickly got the bedpan, pulled down my mother's pants and panties and attempted to have her roll to one side and then onto the bedpan. Mom performed the rolling over and then back with the hopes of landing correctly on the bed pan. That exercise was attempted three times without success. Each time, Mom almost got all her personal parts in the right position.

I finally chimed in, "I'm not sure how much longer she can hold it, and we don't have a change of clothes."

The nurse ran out to get help. A second nurse came in, and this time they got Mom positioned on the bedpan. All I remembered was hearing the older nurse tell Mom to keep her legs spread wide, or she would wet herself.

Now that I had seen more of my parents than any child deserves to, nothing fazed me any longer. I actually understand the dull and blank looks doctors and nurses wear on their faces.

It had been a week since Mom fell. She had a sprained ankle, and her foot was still very swollen. I hired a woman to stay with my parents from five in the evening until seven in the morning in case Mom needed help during the night. Mom was a little unstable on her feet, and now it was even worse. The night help gave me the opportunity to get a good rest, knowing someone was there caring for them.

Mom and Dad's care was getting expensive, and I was beginning to worry about making their money last. My parents had saved their whole lives, but never had expected to live this long.

Every time I called or saw Mom, she asked what happened.

My reply was the same. "You fell, and only you and God know exactly what happened."

Mom quickly replied. "Well, you know, I don't remember, so make sure you ask God."

SURVEY (6/6/2011)

During today's visit I noticed a hospital survey on the table next to Mom's chair. She didn't remember falling or going to the emergency room but that didn't stop her from answering all the survey questions.

She answered "Not sure" to the question: "Did you see a doctor in the emergency room?" Then she responded "No" to "Did you have to wait too long to see a doctor?" She also reported that she only had to wait less than a half hour before seeing a doctor. Our wait for the doctor was over an hour.

I admired her attempt.

MY SISTER (6/11/2011)

Today, I received a call from my cousin. She told me my Dad's sister had called her, concerned about my parents.

My aunt had called Mom and Dad. She spoke to her brother, who didn't know who she was. She was very upset that he had forgotten her.

I called Dad to see what he remembered, if anything, regarding the conversation. His reply was simple and insightful. "Well, if I couldn't hear her, how would I know who she was?"

I was now aware Dad was not only having a problem hearing the TV but hearing over the phone. Mom always answered, so it had not been obvious that he could not hear. I put a hearing-impaired phone on my shopping list.

Jim felt we should buy Dad wireless headphones to help him hear the TV without blasting everyone with the loud volume. He also suggested a new, larger TV with zoom capabilities to help Dad see the screen better.

The next day we went shopping and explained to Dad that our purchases were early Father's Day gifts. He would have had a fit if he knew we spent his money on a new TV.

When we walked into the apartment with the TV and headphones, the TV was so loud I couldn't hear myself think. Mom shouted, "Len, turn down the volume! It's so loud you're going to go deaf."

I thought to myself, *"It's too late, Mom."*

Dad had had the headphones for eleven days now. He answered my morning call with, "Mariann, you know these things you bought me?"

"What things?" I asked.

"Those things you gave me for my ears."

"Oh, you mean the headphones."

"Well, I don't like them, and I don't need them. I can hear fine."

Why was it that, no matter what their age, men refused to admit to a hearing loss? They pretended to hear conversations, smile, and often say, "What was that?"

Dad believed he could hear fine. He was right, if the TV blasted at top volume. I gave up trying to convince him how much better it would be to use the headphones. I returned them, and made an appointment for Dad to see an ear doctor.

At least he was using the hearing impaired phone.

FAMILY REUNION (6/17/2011)

My mother's family had planned a reunion in Connecticut. For days I struggled with whether to leave Mom and Dad for six days and attend. Mom seemed better, and Jim persuaded me that a few days away would do us some good.

On Friday, our first day in Connecticut, Jim's phone rang. His reply to the caller made me uncomfortable: "I'll get Mariann for you."

He handed me the phone, and glancing at the display screen I noticed the call originated from Savannah Seniors. My initial thought was that Mom had fallen again.

The woman on the phone was the physical therapist at the retirement community. She explained that some of the staff were concerned about Mom and suggested physical therapy might help her gait and strengthen her leg muscles. I was relieved and delighted that someone might get Mom walking more.

Monday morning I called Mom and Dad from Connecticut to tell them about the physical therapy and explained that the therapist would be contacting them to get Mom's insurance cards. Mom asked me at least a dozen times to explain what was going on and why she needed the therapist. Finally I got tired of answering the same question.

Abruptly I replied, "Mom, please trust me."

As she was hanging up the phone I could hear her tell my Dad with a sarcastic tone. "Well, I guess we're no longer allowed to ask questions."

I hated to be curt with my mother, and was upset with myself. She didn't intend to provoke me, but her repeating wore me down. I hoped my endurance would last longer.

THE TIME HAS COME (7/7/2011)

I had avoided this day for several months. I blindly wanted to believe my mother could still remember some of the good times we continued to share and those we had already shared. Today, I finally admitted to myself my mother had no short-term memory. I wasn't sure why I took so long to admit that to myself. Maybe because of the pain it gave me or the realization that my mother was no longer the woman she once was.

Often the best part of life was not the actual experience but reliving it over and over again through reminiscing and storytelling. My mother's life had changed. She went through the day without any recollection of what she had recently done, where she had gone, or whom she had seen.

I was trying to adjust to my new mother and learning to enjoy her repeat the stories she could still remember, over and over again.

TOTALLY CONFUSED (7/12/2011)

Just when I had begun to accept that Mom had no short-term memory, a day like today happened.

I arranged to have lunch with Mom and Dad. Mom was ecstatic. She marched into the dining room with a big smile on her face and could not wait to introduce me to everyone. Most of them had been introduced to me at least a dozen times before today. I reminded her before entering the dining room that she didn't have to introduce me to everyone, but she still proceeded with the introductions.

We had a nice lunch, and I tried to keep the conversation light and enjoyable. We spoke mostly about Mom's Bingo, Dad's art class, and my grandchildren.

Driving away, I thought it was too bad Mom would not remember the lunch. Was I ever wrong. I called later in the afternoon, and Mom answered in a happy mood.

"Lunch was so nice today," she said. "Let's do it again soon. I love showing you off to my friends."

When I phoned them after dinner, she still remembered the day. I knew she would forget by tomorrow, but to see the smile on her face made it a wonderful day.

I was puzzled as to why my mother remembered our lunch, but never other occasions. I had been trying to get them out of their routine environment on a weekly basis. The activity varied between visits to our house, breakfast or lunch at their favorite restaurants, a trip to the yogurt shop or a ride through town. My parents never demonstrated the overwhelming excitement with the other outings as they had with our lunch today.

I found the fact that neither one of my parents forgets when it came to paying a bill or depositing money baffling. Mom received a bill from her insurance company two days ago. During lunch, she asked me more than once if I had paid the bill. She even remembered the exact amount owed.

CAN YOU HEAR ME? (7/14/2011)

The time spent in the waiting room to see an ear doctor was shorter than the wait for any other type of doctor.

After I completed the routine paperwork, a young lady called Dad into the examination room.

The doctor checked Dad's ears, and felt a good ear cleaning might help improve Dad's hearing. Both Dad and I winced every time the tweezers-like tool entered his ear to remove wax. I was certain Dad was going to jump right out of the chair every time the doctor moved toward him.

At his age, adjusting to a hearing aid would be difficult. If he couldn't change the batteries in a TV remote control, he wouldn't have a chance with the tiny hearing-aid batteries that needed replacement once a week.

When we got in the car he said to me, "I didn't like that, but I can hear much better."

CHINESE CHECKERS (7/16/2011)

It was a rainy day. Our car was almost at the 120,000-mile mark. Jim decided it was time to begin the "looking-for-a-new-car process," and a rainy day would be as good as any day to start it. Jim enjoyed car shopping. I was too impatient to deal with car salespeople. I decided to visit Mom and Dad while Jim inspected every make and model of SUV on every car lot in Savannah.

Jim dropped me off at my parent's apartment. I knocked on the door. No answer. I turned the doorknob, and it was locked. I wandered down the hall thinking they might be doing their laundry. I peeked in the laundry room, and they were not there, either. I called down to the front desk and asked if they had seen my parents. The receptionist had seen them earlier in the day, but not recently. So I walked back toward the laundry room, this time the ladies playing cards in the activity room next door noticed me and pointed down the hall. My parents were at the end of the hall, sitting on their walkers, resting.

They were glad to see me. I could hear Mom say. "Is that ours?" she pointed to me.

As we walked back to their apartment, we passed a Chinese checkers board all set up in the games area. Mom asked if I knew how to play, I answered her, yes. I sat her down, and we began to play. Playing a game with Mom was fun. I was so pleased she beat me, and she wanted to play again.

"See? I may not remember things, but I'm not stupid."

"Mom, you've never been stupid," I was quick to reply.

We played five games; she won one, I won twice, and we tied twice. Playing with my mother gave me a good feeling. I would never have considered doing this with her. Dad didn't want to play but had fun watching us.

I knew Jim would be hours looking for a car. When the three of us got back to their apartment, I gave Dad a shave.

For more than a year, he had been trying to use an electric razor with little success. He shaved only one side of his face and forgot to shave under his chin and directly below his mouth. My brother thought it would be easier for Dad to use an electric razor. Lenny bought him a new one every time he visited hoping to find one Dad could easily use. Frequently, I ended up giving Dad a shave with a safety razor.

He was pleased with his hairless face and acted as if it were the first time he had been shaved.

"Okay, now all I have to do is push the button on the can and the stuff comes out, put some on my face, shave with the razor, and then wash my face, right?"

He asked me the same question on how to shave three more times. His forgetting how to shave with a safety razor shocked me. I estimated he must have started shaving at eighteen. That would mean that he had probably shaved more than 26,000 times and now had forgotten what to do.

Out of the clear blue, Mom shouted out, "Oh, by the way, I have been made president."

My reaction was excitement to think my mother was selected to be the president of something. "Mom, what were you elected president of?"

"Well, I'm president of the Big Bouncy Boobies Club and my friend is president of the Teeny-Weeny Titties Club," she proclaimed with a smile.

I couldn't stop laughing. When I finally composed myself, Mom confessed one of the staff with very small boobs gave them each the titles. I loved my mother. She lived life with a sense of humor and could laugh at herself.

THE DREADED CALL (7/22/2011)

Jim looked at the caller ID and handed me the phone. "It's from Savannah Seniors."

Since my parents seldom called, my heart sunk. The activities director was calling. She wanted to let me know that the staff was concerned about Dad. This surprised me because he seemed to be doing great lately.

The security guard noticed Dad leaving his used diapers in the laundry room trash can and found one tied up in a pillowcase outside his door. Residents were instructed to leave trash outside their door before going to bed. They were not one hundred percent certain but believed it was Dad who had left the diapers.

The activities director also expressed a concern that during a "popsicle social," Dad claimed not to have a key to his mailbox and insisted his mail was delivered daily to his door.

I appreciated the call and I was glad the staff was paying attention to my parents. I took a deep breath and drove over to see Mom and Dad. The entire ride over I contemplated what I would say to them and decided the direct approach would be the best.

I knocked on the door. They were positioned comfortably in their chairs when I opened the door.

After warm hellos I started. "Dad, where are you putting your used diapers?"

He gave me a baffled look and proceeded to tell me he had run out of trash bags, and was putting the disposable underwear in the laundry room. Anticipating this was the case, I had come with a large box of kitchen trash bags. I sighed with relief.

I questioned him about the mailbox key, and he appeared puzzled when I showed him the key on his key chain. For three years now he had made the daily trip down the hall to his mailbox and now had forgotten.

Whenever I visited my parents, I did what I called the "walk-around" – looking around to find things that didn't seem right.

Mom usually made the bed every day. My grandmother used to tell me a house looked messy when your bed was not made, and making a bed only took a few minutes. Today the bed had not been made, so I made it. I noticed stains on the bed-sheets. I read that people with memory problems often lose bladder control. I asked Mom what happened, never really expecting her to remember. Her answer was, "I don't know how that got there. I didn't do it."

I feared the day when I have to tell my parents they needed to move to assisted living but I knew that day was approaching. Mom viewed assisted living as the step before dying. A friend of mine told me my parents were able to live independently for so long because I was their assisted living. Her words resonated in my brain. She was right. I hoped we could put off the transfer to assisted living until we sold our house and moved to Charleston.

A GOOD DAY (8/7/2011)

Jim and I were out shopping and decided to surprise my parents and join them for lunch. Mom beamed when she saw us and smiled all through lunch.

As we left she thanked us.

"This was a perfect day. What could be better than having lunch with the ones you love?"

REMEMBER 911 (8/11/2011)

This weekend was my daughter's thirty-fifth birthday. Jim and I made plans weeks ago to go to Charleston. We were going to watch our grandchildren on Friday night while Marisa and Ricardo went out to dinner. On Saturday, I planned to take my daughter on a birthday shopping spree.

Jim and I decided to go up to Charleston on Wednesday and house hunt.

Adhering to my usual routine, on Wednesday night I called Mom and Dad after dinner. Mom answered and sounded distracted. Then I heard Mom talking to Dad. "Len, are you sick?"

"Mom, what's wrong with Pop?"

"I don't know. He said he's okay."

I decided to call back in fifteen minutes. I was hoping his problem was a little indigestion from dinner.

When I called back, Mom answered again, and I could hear someone talking in the background.

"Mom, who's that talking?"

"I'm not sure, but he's talking to your Dad."

I asked to speak with the person and found out Dad complained he wasn't feeling well when he left the dining room after dinner.

The fellow I spoke to was a staff member who decided to check up on Dad. He had also called Security, who called a nurse on staff.

By that time I was certain Dad was having a heart attack.

I kept asking if Dad was having chest pains and instructed the security guard to give him a nitroglycerin pill kept in the refrigerator.

Keeping calm was not happening as I tried to ask what was going on. All I remembered was the security guard telling me he had called 911, and the emergency vehicle was on the way. He promised to call me when the EMTs arrived.

After what seemed like forever but was probably only ten minutes, an EMT called me. I tried to answer all his medical questions.

At that point I gave myself a "to do" item and promised myself I'd write down my parents' medical and prescription information and leave a copy on their refrigerator.

We left everything and started the two-and-a-half-hour drive back to Savannah. I called wonderful friends who went to the hospital and stayed with Mom and Dad until we got there.

When we arrived at the emergency room, Mom was sitting on her walker positioned right by Dad's bed. I was shocked that the driver had been able to get her into the truck. Standing no taller than four feet ten inches, she had difficulty getting into our SUV.

The doctor ran several tests and found nothing wrong with Dad. Dad insisted he felt fine. At midnight, we were driving home. Mom and Dad were tired and happy to be home. Mom was confused as to why we were all out so late.

Early the following morning, Jim and I decided to check on Dad. When we got to their apartment, they were dressed and had already eaten breakfast. Dad gave us a big, "Good morning."

"How do you feel, Pop?" I inquired.

"Good, I feel good, and I'm heading downstairs for men's club," he answered as he started out the door.

Jim turned to me and said, "Why the hell did we come home?"

All I could do was shake my head.

Mom didn't even remember going to the emergency room. I guess sometimes having dementia might be a blessing. They both seemed rested, and Jim and I were exhausted as we drove back to Charleston.

DON'T TOUCH ME (8/16/2011)

While checking in on my parents today, I decided it would be a good time for pedicures and a hair cut for Dad. Lately I've noticed his sensitivity to touch. He pulled away if I touched his feet, fingers, or face. Cutting his nails had become a tug-of-war. I tried to hold his finger, and he pulled away as the clipper got closer.

I was curious as to why he would be doing this, so I asked their doctor's nurse about his behavior.

She explained people with dementia become more sensitive to touch. I was learning something new about my parents every day.

WATER (8/20/2011)

We arranged to take Mom and Dad out to breakfast this morning. Our downstairs air conditioner was not working, so it was off to our favorite breakfast spot.

Last night Dad brought up something about water on the kitchen floor and asked if I would bring them paper towels. I suggested he look in the cabinet to the left of the stove, where I had put four rolls. He insisted he looked all over and did not have any.

On the drive over to breakfast, I mentioned to Dad that I had brought four paper-towel rolls for him.

He was happy and added, "There is still water on the floor."

"Dad, why haven't you called anyone?" I questioned.

"I don't know who to call, so I'm telling you."

After breakfast, we went to check out the water. Dad was right. An inch of water was covering the kitchen floor.

I was surprised neither one of them had fallen.

I called the maintenance man on duty, and he found a cracked hose leading into the ice maker. He mopped up the water and solved the problem.

I opened the kitchen cabinets to put away the paper towels, and right in front of me were four rolls of paper towels. I pointed this out to my parents and asked them to double-check each other next time.

As usual, Mom was the one with the quick reply. "Thank you for your advice. I'll take it into consideration," with that she rolled her eyes.

Jim could not stop laughing.

ONE MORE TIME (8/21/2011)

We had just sat down to watch the nightly news when the phone rang. As I picked up the receiver to see who was calling, my stomach fell to the floor. The call originated from my parents' retirement community.

The receptionist wanted me to know they had called 911 for Dad. He experienced dizziness again at dinner and felt nauseated.

Jim and I immediately drove over. I called along the way to get a status report, and the receptionist informed me the emergency crew had left. Dad's vital signs were good, and he refused to go to the hospital.

When we arrived, Dad looked fine but a little pale.

Lately getting any information from my parents had become difficult. Mom's short-term memory was gone, and Dad was starting to forget as well. Neither one could remember if they had eaten lunch or had drunk anything since breakfast. I gave Dad some crackers and a drink. He proceeded to tell us he was fine but wanted to take a nap so we should go home.

We left. I was learning to control my urge to panic.

THE DAY WILL COME (8/22/2011)

I called my parents early this morning. Mom answered the phone. "Hi, Mom. How's Pop?"

"I'm very well, thank you," she answered in a sarcastic voice.

"Mom, I'm asking about Pop because he felt sick last night, and 911 was called."

"Oh, just kidding. He's fine."

Sometimes she acted so childish. I found her attitude rather interesting. She was jealous over my concern for Dad.

Dad got on the phone. "I'm fine and going to art class at ten-thirty, bye."

Later in the day my uncle called to see how Dad was doing. He was my mother's youngest brother and had been a second Dad to me and my brother. He also asked how I was doing.

"The best I can," I answered.

He mentioned that it might be time for Mom and Dad to move into assisted living, and it would be okay if they did. I was relieved to hear this from him. For some reason having his approval would make the assisted living decision easier when the time came, and I knew it was approaching soon.

I hadn't cried much during the last three years and had tried to stay strong for all of us. The idea of having my parents move to assisted living made me cry. I viewed it as signifying the end of their life, but I knew their increasing care needs would end up taking over my life. I couldn't let that happen.

BIG (8/24/2011)

Dad had an appointment to get blood work done. I convinced Mom to stay home because we would be back within an hour. I called to check on her while Dad was in the lab. She answered the phone completely out of breath.

"Mom, are you okay?"

"I'm fine. I can't get this damn bra hooked. Your father usually does it for me."

"He'll be home soon, so wait."

When we got back, Mom was still sitting on the bed, bra opened at the front, waiting to be hooked.

Little did I know I was about to share this experience with my cousin from Connecticut. She called me later in the day. She was laughing as she said, "I have to tell you about the conversation I had with your mother today."

She must have called my mother about the same time I did this morning.

"Your Mom answered the phone all out of breath and explained that she was having trouble hooking her bra."

Mom said to her, "You know I've gotten really big. I mean my boobs have gotten really big. It's a shame I can't put them to good use and make some money from them and share them with the world. You know there's enough to go around for everyone."

I admired my mother. She had always been able to go through life laughing at herself but never at others.

When she was much younger, I asked if she would consider breast reduction. She did not hesitate to reply.

"Well, if God wanted me to go through life with small boobs He would have made me that way. This is how He made me, so why would I want to change anything?"

SEE YOU IN A YEAR, MAYBE (8/26/2011)

This trip to the urologist was the best yet, if a trip to the urologist could ever be good.

Dad and I went to the restroom together. After I helped him pull down his pants and diaper, he deposited a respectable sample in the cup and did it in a relatively short time.

The doctor came into the examination room, smiling, and gave us a pleasant greeting. I asked if he remembered us and the "target" on his back. He smiled and said, "Oh, yes."

He proceeded to inform me that there was still some blood in Dad's urine but not enough to be concerned about. He also explained Dad's bladder could be scanned for tumors, but … Before he could finish his sentence I asked, "What's the point?"

His response was simple. "Right. What's the point?"

I knew that even if Dad had tumors, I would not put him through any painful procedures or treatments at ninety years old.

I inquired about Dad sleeping in his chair. The doctor said it wasn't unusual for older people to be more comfortable sleeping in an upright position.

The doctor shook Dad's hand. "See you in a year."

"Yeah, see you in a year, if I'm still around," Dad replied.

"Me, too," the doctor answered.

MEAN MARY (8/27/2011)

"Len, you're so stupid. Hurry up! Pick up the extension phone. It's Mariann. Didn't you hear it ring? You could have picked it up, but you're so lazy."

I never heard my mother so mean and critical about anyone, let alone my father.

I had read that people with memory loss often go through an ambivalent and mean period. Her lack of memory had to be causing her stress and fear.

I knew Mom was frustrated by her dependency on my father and me. She was angry over the reality of no longer remembering. Her irritability never lasted long. I was troubled when she treated Dad nastily. He was a good husband, and never responded to her harsh words. I hoped she didn't become Mean Mary.

THE SIGNS (8/28/2011)

The *USA Weekend* magazine in the paper today had an article written by Madonna Behen, titled "Signs of Alzheimer's vs. Typical Age-related Changes."

It cited the following differences:

Poor judgment and decision-making vs. making a bad decision once in a while.

Inability to manage a budget vs. missing a monthly payment.

Losing track of the date or the season vs. forgetting which day it is and remembering later.

Difficulty having a conversation vs. sometimes forgetting which word to use.

Misplacing things and being unable to retrace steps to find them vs. losing things from time to time.

Mom demonstrated signs from both columns, but most of her signs were from the Alzheimer's side. I hated to read this, but I had known all along she was getting worse. I prayed Mom wouldn't forget me.

I guess I kept trying to get through to her because I loved her. It was hard to stop because I didn't want to lose her.

The article also listed seven items that helped the memory. I went to visit and showed her a section headed "Take a Walk."

"Mom, read number six in this article: research indicates physical activity is beneficial for your brain and your body." I proposed we go for a walk.

"No, not now. I'm tired," she stated. I was hoping she was listening to me.

"How old am I? Almost eighty-eight, right? Well, would you be happy living to eighty-eight?"

"Yes," I said answering honestly.

"Well, I am too, so I don't feel like walking."

In *Coastal Senior* was an article titled "Sharing a Few Senior Laughs" by Bess Chappas. One of the quips sounded just like my mother.

"Every time I hear the dirty word *exercise,* I wash my mouth out with chocolate."

I knew if I promised Mom chocolate at the end of the walk, she probably would have been more agreeable.

RABBIT (9/1/2011)

The phone rang at seven-thirty this morning. Being the anxious person I am, I figured it was a call about Mom and Dad. I was wrong. It was our five-year-old granddaughter.

Her conversation started with a loud, "Rabbit!" A big laugh followed.

My daughter said our granddaughter was learning about the calendar, and on her way to school said, "Mommy, today is September first."

My daughter immediately thought about my father and his rabbit tradition and decided she would have our granddaughter call us and continue the tradition. It started our day off right.

THE CHAIR (9/2/2011)

I concluded if Dad wanted to sleep in a chair it should be a comfortable one and small enough to fit in his bedroom. That way he could still sleep next to Mom.

I searched online to get an understanding of features and prices. Jim and I planned to go to several stores to find a good chair that would not break the bank, and the simpler to use the better. More features meant more confusion.

Jim insisted we check them out in person and try them for comfort. So off we went to medical supply stores and several furniture stores.

The La-Z-Boy recliners were great chairs but more expensive than I planned to spend. As the manager of my parents' finances, I wanted their money to last as long as they did. The saleswoman at La-Z-Boy was very helpful, but I made it clear the chairs were out of our price range. She proceeded to explain the chairs came with a lifetime guarantee. When I reminded her Dad was ninety, she laughed and said, "I guess the guarantee is not really important to you."

At the medical supply store, we bought Dad a lift chair and scheduled to have it delivered that afternoon. The chair was a motorized recliner that is constructed to lift a person to almost a standing position. The chair had two buttons - an up arrow for the standing position and a down arrow for sitting and reclining.

Jim and I could not be at my parents' apartment for the delivery, but I stressed to Mom and Dad numerous times that afternoon when the chair would be dropped off.

I called again at five to make sure the chair arrived. Dad answered the phone and when he heard it was me asked, "What did this cost me?"

I assured him not to worry about the price, and we would see him tomorrow.

First thing the next morning the phone rang. It was Dad. "I don't want this chair. Take it back."

He was adamant but would not give me a reason why he didn't like the chair. His reason for feeling so strongly about returning the chair took me a while to figure out. Then it dawned on me; he must have seen the sales receipt. I advised Dad returning the chair would have to wait until after the weekend since we had two birthdays to celebrate.

Marisa, Ricardo, Isabella and Dante came for the weekend to celebrate my mother and granddaughter's birthdays. We all went over to pick up Mom and Dad.

Jim and Ricardo were determined they could teach Dad how to use the two control buttons on the chair and convince him to love it.

They guided Dad to the chair and directed him to practice, pushing the up and down buttons. He performed this activity dozens of times until they felt Dad could do it without help.

As soon as the teaching lesson was over, my grandchildren jumped onto the chair and took turns pressing the buttons. They laughed as the chair went down into the recline position and up as it lifted the seat almost pushing them off. Dad enjoyed watching them and joined in their laughter.

I had become a reasonably good liar when it came to telling my parents the cost of items. I told Dad the chair came from our church thrift store and cost me twenty dollars. He was happy to hear that, but I'm not sure he believed me.

We had a great birthday celebration dinner at our house.

When we dropped Mom and Dad home, he promised he would try sleeping in the chair.

MY CHAIR/DAMN CHAIR (9/4/2011)

I had come to the conclusion that as people got older, it was a waste of time and energy to reason with them. I had decided to stop trying to understand the mind of someone over the age of ninety.

During my morning call, Dad picked up the phone. "I love this chair."

I almost fell off of my chair hearing those words.

What started out as a good thing was becoming a nightmare. Every other day Dad either loved or hated the chair.

It was probably a mistake not to have taken him to try the chair, but I knew if he saw the price he would have immediately said no. He saw the price tag when the chair was delivered but I removed it the next day and by now he didn't remember seeing it.

He announced the chair hurt his back, and he would rather sleep in *his* old chair. His chair was sixty-one years old and had been reupholstered at least four times. I didn't think it was very comfortable, but after all those years it had been molded in the shape of Dad's backside.

Mom kept asking how much the new chair cost. I decided to switch strategies and put a different cost on the chair. Two hundred dollars sounded good. The price was a quarter of the actual cost but expensive enough for my mother to insist Dad give the chair a try.

HAPPY BIRTHDAY, I THINK (9/8/2011)

Today Mom turned eighty-eight.

"I can't believe I made it to be this old," she repeated all day long.

We took Mom and Dad out for a birthday dinner celebration. Lately they have had a difficult time finishing their dinners. Dad ate all his fried shrimp, one taste of mashed potatoes, and none of his broccoli. Mom was able to eat most of the french fries and only half of her chicken breast.

After a nice dinner, we went back to their apartment for birthday cake. Neither one had a problem finishing their piece of ice cream cake.

As she blew out the candles, Mom said, "I hope to live another year."

"You will if you walk very day," I said.

With a smile she said, "Well, that's the plan, but, well, I don't have a plan, and if I did, I probably won't stick to it."

Mom looked at all the birthday cards on the table by her chair. She never remembered opening any of them or the happy-birthday phone calls she received from several relatives.

THE REMOTE (9/14/2011)

Tomorrow we are going to babysit for our grandchildren in Charleston.

I made a paper delivery to Mom and Dad's apartment before we left – the usual toilet tissues and adult diapers. Walking out of their bedroom, I overheard Mom talking to Dad.

"Was the TV on all night?"

"Yes," he answered. "I didn't know how to turn it off, so I called downstairs and let them know the TV is broken."

"Where's the remote?" I questioned.

"We don't have a remote."

I found the remote under his footstool and turned off the TV.

"That's great," Dad replied. "I didn't know we had one, and that it worked like that."

Dad had probably been using a TV remote control for more than twenty years.

I'M SICK (9/15/2011)

At seven-thirty this morning, Jim's phone had rung. We were in Charleston helping Marisa with the children because Ricardo was out of town on a business trip. I could tell by the expression on his face the call was not a wrong phone number.

"Hi, Mary. What's wrong?" Jim handed me the phone as he said, "Here's Mariann."

I knew it could not be good news.

She explained Dad didn't feel good. I asked to speak to him. He expressed to me that he didn't have chest pains but could not articulate what was wrong. I told him to get some water and eat a few crackers.

I called back in ten minutes, and he was fine. I checked on him all day, and he was not having any problems. I'm pleased with myself for not panicking.

GO, BRAVES (9/18/2011)

Jim and I were returning on Sunday from our annual weekend trip to Atlanta to cheer on the Braves. It was a great weekend with our team winning yesterday one to nothing over the New York Mets.

The Braves were playing the Mets again today. We decided to pick up Mom and Dad on our way home, and take them to our house to watch the game on TV.

Jim dropped me off in front of their building, and I went in to get my parents. I'd called them earlier, so I expected them to be ready. When I got to the second floor, they were in the hall heading toward the elevator. I noticed the manager on duty calling them back toward their apartment. I figured something was wrong.

I found out that Mom had reported her ring missing and the manager was coming to help her find it. "They" hadn't taken anything in quite a while. I thanked the manager and informed her I would look for it.

I had tried several times to convince Mom to wear another less expensive ring but a major conflict took place. Again I started the search with my prayer to St. Anthony and as expected I found it in five minutes under her bed.

As I bent down to look under the bed, I noticed a large brownish/yellow spot on the floor. I stopped asking Mom how the stains got there. She didn't remember and blamed the mess on someone else. I got so discouraged and tired when I faced this type of situation.

Mom would be mortified if she knew what she was doing. To make matters worse, I recently had their carpet cleaned.

I called Jim who was patiently waiting in the car, and let him know we were going to be detained. I recommended he wait for us in the residents' TV room.

With cleaning supplies in hand I started working on the stain.

"Don't worry about the cleaning. I can do it or the cleaning lady will take care of whatever you're doing," Mom said.

If she only knew the mess I had to clean.

Dad also greeted me with a surprise. He was sporting a five-day beard. The hair above his lip could not be called a "mustache;"

it was more like an "advertisement" for everything he had eaten in the last several days. I got out the razor and shaving cream and proceeded once again to teach Dad how to shave.

After cleaning and shaving we only had time for a drive around town which pleased them both.

STRONG WILLED (9/20/2011)

I was doing my best, but lately my caregiver role had been taking a toll on me. I was having trouble finding humor to help me cope with the stress. Sometimes what kept me going was Mom and Dad's sincere appreciation for all my help.

I was desperately trying to put off the assisted-living decision for their sake and mine. From what I had observed over the last few years, as soon as someone moved into assisted living, their spirit changed and the person died shortly thereafter. My resistance to assisted-living probably stemmed from this observation.

Mom had already said several times. "I'm going to will myself to die before I rely on a stranger to take care of me."

I decided to talk to them about the situation. I sat them down, turned off the TV, made sure they were focusing on me, and began the conversation.

"You know I love you both very much."

"We love you more," Mom chimed in.

I explained that I could not do everything for them and needed their cooperation. I went on by saying unless they did their laundry and cared for themselves, like shaving every day, they would have to move to the assisted-living section.

Simultaneously, they turned to look at each other and said, "Okay."

TIMES ARE CHANGING (9/21/2011)

I opened their apartment door and received a big greeting, and much to my surprise Dad had as clean a shaved face as I had seen in months.

I insisted Dad change the shirt he had worn since Sunday. I helped him take off the shirt and noticed his T-shirt had yellow stains on the front and back. If I were to guess, the spots were urine, but I didn't detect any odor. I also insisted he put on a clean T-shirt. I went over to his dresser to get him one. Every T-shirt he owned had large yellow stains in the front and back. The only conclusion that made any sense was he tucked the T-shirts into the Depends. I left him two T-shirts. These were the least stained and threw out the rest.

As soon as he had put on the clean shirt, I heard him say, "I can't find my watch."

Once again I petitioned St. Anthony's help. I knew it had to be close by. I looked in his chair, under the chair, on the table near his chair, in the bathroom, on his bed, on his night table, and in his pockets, but still no watch.

I knew Dad was wearing the watch prior to changing his shirt because he asked me to reset it for him. I was beside myself. I'm not sure why I did this, but I felt Dad's arm. Of course, the watch was on his arm halfway between his wrist and elbow. We all laughed, and Dad shouted out, "I'll be damned!"

"You never know what to expect with old people," Mom declared.

IN SEARCH OF NEMO (9/25/2011)

My daughter called this afternoon to share a conversation my five-year-old granddaughter had with my mother.

"How old are you?" Mom asked.

"I'm five."

A few minutes later my Mom asked her again, "How old are you?"

"Gigi, I told you: I'm five. Do you have short-term memory loss?" my granddaughter replied.

My daughter, who was listening to the conversation, could not believe what she was hearing. When the conversation ended, Marisa questioned my granddaughter and asked where she learned about "short-term memory loss."

Her reply was simple. "I learned it from Dory in the *Nemo* movie."

I went back and looked at the movie segment where Dory showed Marlin the way to the boat that took Nemo. Marlin was confused by Dory's actions and asks, "What's going on here?"

"I'm so sorry. See, I suffer from short-term memory loss. I forget things almost instantly. It runs in my family. Well, at least I think it does ... hmm," Dory replied.

Needless to say I was proud of my granddaughter. I thought it was extremely intelligent for a five-year-old to associate what she saw in a movie to real life. Most of all, I was so grateful for the good laugh, and I hoped the memory loss didn't run in *my* family.

RECALL (9/27/2011)

Today while getting dressed, I had a realization. My Mom had no short-term memory, but she was smart enough to get through her day using recall. For example, I would ask her how Dad's toe had been doing since he had his nails cut.

"What about his toe?" she inquired

I would proceed by telling her we went to the podiatrist, and then out to lunch.

"Oh, yes, I'm sure his toe is fine, and it is always great to be with you," was her response.

She remembered nothing of the day but still recalled the appropriate way to respond.

UNTIL DEATH DO US PART (9/28/2011)

Wow! Mom and Dad were married sixty-two years ago today. That's longer than I had been living.

The life experiences they had gone through together were too numerous to list: wars, the Great Depression, marriage, raising children, technology changes, political upheaval, deaths, and the list goes on.

I was proud of them. Marriage wasn't always easy, though growing up I remembered very few times they didn't get along.

Dad's temper did not flair often, but when it did he would shout how he felt and then quickly apologized. Mom would hold her own and was quick to forgive. Their faith in God, love for their family, and their commitment to their marriage kept them strong.

Having gone through two marriages - the first one lasting almost seven years and the second going strong at thirteen years - I found it difficult to understand the bond between my parents. I was positive there were times neither one wanted to go on but hung in there because they didn't want to leave the other alone. They needed each other.

My mother had always said, "I don't know what I would do without your father. I pray we die together."

Mom and I shared the same prayer.

When I called to wish them Happy Anniversary, Mom answered the phone.

"Hi, Mom, how are you and Pop doing this morning?" It was now eleven in the morning.

"We're doing fine. I'm helping your Dad dress."

"Mom, I'm sorry. Do you want me to get someone in to help you do that?"

"Why? Didn't I say for better or worse?"

"That's why I'm calling – to wish you a Happy Anniversary."

"It's our anniversary?" she questioned. "Hey, Len, did you remember it's our anniversary?"

"No."

Jim and I had dinner with them. I asked Dad if he would marry Mom again, and he shouted, "Yes!"

She quickly answered, "What do you expect him to say? He has no choice. He's got me, and he has to keep me."

THE SHOWER (9/29/2011)

This morning I stopped by to drop off some paper supplies. My parents had been leaving their door unlocked lately - something my mother would never have done in the past.

I walked in calling, "Hello?" and saw Dad coming out of the bedroom.

He was happy to see me and informed me, "Your mother is in the bathroom."

I noticed a large stain on the carpet about a foot in diameter near the bathroom door.

Walking closer, I realized water was coming from the bathroom. I yelled to my mother and asked what she was doing.

"I'm going to take a shower, but there is water all over the floor."

The first thing that entered my mind was her falling on the floor, followed quickly with, why is she showering alone? Even though they lived in an independent facility, limited assisted-living services were offered at a charge. I had arranged for them to get assistance in the shower, and posted signs in the bathroom reminding them of the shower days.

Before my mind finished collecting my thoughts the bathroom door opened and there was Mom standing in front of me, naked.

If that wasn't enough of a surprise, I looked down at the floor, which was covered by at least three inches of water. I wouldn't call maintenance for help, with Mom standing there in her birthday suit, and I didn't want her to move fearing she might slip.

I gathered every towel in the bathroom and used them to create a walkway. I got Mom into the bedroom without a fall and proceeded to mop up the water. It took me forty-five minutes to clean up the mess. I was mentally and physically exhausted.

Naturally, Mom had no recollection of what happened. My guess was she turned the shower on, left the shower door open, and pointed the hand-held nozzle out, allowing the water to run all over the floor.

By the time I finished, Mom was dressed.

Before leaving, I hung a large sign on their bathroom mirror, high enough to be out of reach. It read, do not shower alone.

BIRTHDAY TRIP (10/2/2011)

Today was Jim's birthday, and we decided to take a weeklong sailing trip. I intentionally did not tell Mom and Dad how long we planned to be away. Mom would get very anxious if she knew we were out of town.

Every day when I called, I told them we were no more than an hour away and on our way home. This conversation went on for more than a week. We had a great trip, and Mom and Dad were fine for the entire time.

THE STRAITJACKET (10/18/2011)

Dad was having difficulty putting on pullover sweaters. I bought him two new zip-up sweatshirts. I had him try one on, and he loved it.

I called today.

Dad answered the phone. "You need to take the sweatshirt back."

"I thought you liked it."

"The one in the bag doesn't fit."

"Dad, it's the same size and style as the one you wore yesterday. I don't understand."

Raising his voice, he said, "Take it back. It doesn't fit!"

I was anxious to understand what was wrong with the sweatshirt and decided to drive over to see for myself.

I pulled the sweatshirt out of the bag and asked Dad to try it on. He put one arm in and seemed to be having a little problem with the other arm but finally had both arms in the sweatshirt.

"See? It doesn't fit right," he said.

I couldn't answer him because I was laughing to the point of tears. Dad had not completely unzipped the sweatshirt before putting it on. He slipped his arms through so the bulk of the jacket was behind him, still zipped. He looked like he was wearing an inverted straitjacket. He was amazed when I unzipped the sweatshirt, and it fit.

MY WATCH (10/23/2011)

Dad's watch decided to get lost again. I was getting so good at finding lost items; I may start a business offering lost-and-found services to retirement and assisted-living communities.

Dad told me he looked all over for his watch, and I would never find it, so I should buy him a new one.

One quick look on his recliner saved me a trip to the store. Thank you, St. Anthony!

I LOST IT (11/2/2011)

In the past three years, I have "lost it" once before today.

The first time was a few months ago at the Veterans Administration office. I learned that Dad, having served in World War II, was eligible for an Aid and Attendance pension from the Veterans Administration. I spent six months working on Dad's application, making sure I had all the correct medical and financial information documented as requested.

Once the application was completed, the next step was a meeting with a Veterans Administration representative to review the application.

I arrived at the administration office thirty minutes before they opened, optimistically thinking I would be the first in line. What a silly assumption. The place was packed, and five people had signed in before me. I waited five hours to be notified the person I wanted to see had to leave early. This meant I had to go through the same exercise again on Monday.

I wasn't sure what came over me, but as I walked to my car, I broke down and started to cry uncontrollably.

The gentleman I was waiting to see happened to be walking out of the building behind me. I hurried my pace to avoid him seeing my tears.

He called out to me, "Ma'am, ma'am! Were you waiting to see me?"

I didn't want anyone to see me so distraught, but I could not ignore him. I tried answering him while still three steps ahead, and he caught up with me.

He apologized for not being able to see me and asked why I was there. I blurted out something about Dad, Mom, and me their caregiver. I wasn't exactly sure what I said, but I remembered being hugged and comforted by a stranger. He promised that I would be his first appointment on Monday morning.

I returned on Monday and met with the kind man who had given me that much-needed hug. He processed Dad's application.

Today I had my second meltdown. Mom had a doctor's appointment this morning at ten-thirty. I called at eight-forty to remind her. She was still in bed. I instructed her to get washed and dressed, and informed her I was coming to pick her up at ten, downstairs. She assured me she would be ready and shouted to Dad, "I need to get up and ready for my doctor's appointment."

Mom wasn't waiting downstairs when I arrived, so I parked the car and ran upstairs to their apartment.

As I opened the apartment door and walked in, I saw no sign of Mom or Dad. I shouted, "Hello?" The reply came from the bedroom, "Who's there?"

Walking into the bedroom, my mother was still in bed in her nightgown, and Dad was sitting in his bedside chair, fully dressed. All I could do was shake my head in disbelief and shout, "Why aren't you dressed and ready to go?"

"Go where?" Mom asked.

It was too late to get mom dressed and to the doctor's office in time to make her appointment. I called the doctor to cancel. The doctor's nurse was wonderful. She said she understood and managed to get Mom in for an afternoon appointment.

Later that day Mom and I made the trip to the doctor. Everything went well except Mom's weight. She had gained thirty-five pounds in three years. She insisted both the doctor and I were lying about her weight. I was agitated and asked her why I would lie to her.

"Well, I'm not sure why you would lie to me, but I know I have always been this weight."

I COULD DANCE ALL NIGHT (11/23/2011)

On my way to see my parents, I ran into the manager of the Savannah Seniors. He gave me a pleasant hello followed by, "How are your parents doing?"

I thought about his question and turned my answer into a question. "You tell me. I'm here often but don't see them every day like you do."

He hesitated momentarily. "Good. They are doing well, but I worry about their stability. Your father gives me a heart attack every time he gets up and dances. Maybe some time in rehabilitation would be good for them."

"By 'rehabilitation' do you mean assisted living?" I asked myself, *"What is he talking about?"* I inquired if anyone had moved into assisted-living and then moved back to independent living.

I knew what he would say, so I replied, "I know the day is coming soon, but I'd like to keep them here as long as possible for their well-being and mine. I respect your opinion and if you really think they should move, I will do it."

He nodded and said, "I understand. We'll let you know when the time is right for a move."

I FEEL SORRY FOR MYSELF (12/5/2011)

My conversations with Mom were getting shorter and shorter. I stopped asking, "What did you do today?"

I knew the answer would be, "I don't remember. Let me ask your father." She always added, "You know I have no memory, and I used to be so sharp."

I learned to share with her my day and stories about my grandchildren. This kept her relaxed and not pressured into pretending to remember daily events.

Accepting that I could no longer have a meaningful conversation with my mother was difficult. I missed this more than anything. We used to talk daily. She shared my joys, listened to my problems without interruption, helped me resolve issues without passing judgment, and gave me advice when asked. Mom was my best friend.

I'M NOT ALONE (12/17/2011)

For the past week Dad had reminded me that I needed to talk with his art teacher. Actually, he reminded me every time I'd seen or called them this week.

I contacted her today, and she asked if I would get Dad a plastic pencil case for his paints. A case would make it easier for him to access his paints. He had been carrying them in a tote bag.

Walking into Walmart, I felt like a mother buying school supplies for her child. I chose a ninety-nine cent blue pencil case for him.

I placed the case in one of the bags I had in the backseat of the car. The four bags contained my parents' weekly shopping: a large box of Depends, soap, toilet paper, three prescriptions, and the pencil case.

Mom and Dad were happy to see Jim and me. I was in the process of unpacking their supplies when Mom, sitting at the kitchen table finishing her lunch, blurted out, "I'm no good anymore! I don't remember anything, and I think my time to die has come."

I didn't know what to say and decided to make a joke. "Mom, could you wait until after Christmas?"

She was quick to say, "I think so. We're going to see the babies for Christmas, right? I'll wait."

After much convincing, Mom agreed to take a walk with Dad, Jim and me.

A friend of Jim's and mine from church moved into the nursing home on the first floor of my parents' building. He was there to recuperate after a fall that resulted in a broken hip.

We decided to go visit him. His room was empty, so we went to look outside. He was sitting in the gazebo, hand-in-hand with his wife, who had Alzheimer's, along with their daughter, son-in-law, and two nurses. His wife was still living in their home with a full-time nurse. We walked up the stairs into the gazebo. After introductions, Dad and our friend shared information about where they were stationed during World War II, and Mom was exchanging words with his wife. The conversation was soon forgotten by both women.

Our friend's daughter looked stressed. I knew her father was unhappy about being in a nursing home and wanted to go home. We began a conversation, and she explained the struggle she was having trying to decide what to do with her parents. "I keep asking them what they want to do."

All I could say to her was, "Your parents can no longer make good decisions. Do what's best for you and try not to feel guilty once you make the decision."

MERRY CHRISTMAS (12/25/2011)

I wrestled with the pros and cons of taking my parents to Charleston for Christmas. Removing them from their daily routine concerned me, and the possibility that one of them might not make it to the bathroom in time was troubling. I discussed the situation with Jim and Marisa. They agreed that having Mom and Dad celebrate the holiday with family outweighed any issues that might arise.

Jim loaded their clothes, pills, diapers, and toiletries into the car, and mounted their walkers on the bicycle rack. I think we're the only people that have two walkers instead of bicycles mounted on the back of the car. We spent hours looking for a bicycle rack suitable for hauling two walkers.

Fortunately the trip was uneventful, and the rest stop reasonably quick.

When we arrived at my daughter and son-in-law's house, Dad took the nine steps leading to the front porch with ease. Seeing his great-grandchildren smiling and waiting at the front door gave him an extra boost of adrenalin.

Mom, whose extra weight had caused shortness of breath, also made it up the stairs without any problems.

Dad was very talkative during Christmas Eve and Christmas Day dinners. He frequently interrupted the conversation with, "Do you remember ..." or "Whatever happened to ..." or "Remember when we ...." At one point he hollered, "My daughter has a list on our refrigerator of everything that's wrong with us." That had us all laughing so hard my side hurt.

Mom kept saying, "I'm so happy to be with people I love."

After three wonderful days, I was glad we made the trip. What a blessed and memorable Christmas. We may have all thought it might be the last one we would have together.

CHAPTER 6
MOVING ON

FOREVER A MOTHER (1/5/2012)

I contracted some bug over the holidays and felt under the weather. When I called, Mom answered the phone. "Do you have a cold? You don't sound good at all."

"I don't feel that great," I replied.

"When I feel sick, I drink plenty of water and get to bed early. Chicken soup helps too. You need to take care of yourself. I hate to see one of my kids sick."

I immediately felt better hearing my mother sound like she was in charge and suggesting what I should do.

"Thanks, Mom. I think I'll get some water and go straight to bed."

I did just that and found comfort in taking my mother's advice.

TIME TO CRY (1/8/2012)

Jim suggested we have Mom and Dad over for breakfast.

We picked them up after church. They were ready and waiting for us outside in front of their building.

Jim's blueberry pancakes were great, and they enjoyed the visit.

Upon our return to their apartment, I decided to do a walk-about. It had become a habit. The first room I checked was the bathroom and pulled out a Clorox wipe to remove Dad's yellow stains from in front of the toilet bowl.

This time, as I walked in the bathroom, I was not prepared for what I saw. It looked like someone dropped several water balloons from the ceiling, but instead of water it was a *shitty* liquid mixture. The walls, floor, fixtures, and everything else in the bathroom were coated.

I was uncertain as to why I didn't break down and cry. Mom kept asking me over and over what I was doing.

It took me an hour to clean up the mess. I never asked, never wanted to know what happened, and it never occurred again.

91 YEARS (1/21/2012)

We gave Dad the choice of going out for dinner or coming to our house to celebrate his ninety-first birthday. He chose our house.

I've determined the best food to prepare for my father is anything that does not require a lot of chewing. He loves pasta, so pasta it was, followed by an ice-cream cake.

Before dinner we arranged a Skype video call with my daughter and her family. Dad was so happy to see his great-grandchildren.

During dinner, Jim asked Dad if there was anything in his life that he would change. Dad thought for awhile, and responded, "I can't think of anything I would change. I would even marry my wife again." He turned to Mom and gave her a big smile.

NATURAL BEAUTY (1/22/2012

Today was Thursday and Mom's day to get her hair done. When I called I asked her, "Do you look beautiful?"

"No, I don't." After a long pause she proclaimed, "I look gorgeous." She still had her sense of humor.

TOILET BARS (2/3/2012)

To assist Mom and Dad, Jim had installed toilet seat grab bars.

Dad notified Maintenance that the bars were loose. The grab bars were mounted between the toilet bowl and the toilet seat. The bars provided stability when sitting or rising from the toilet.

While visiting, I checked to make sure the grab bars were tightened. I was shocked that the maintenance man had re-installed the grab bars incorrectly – they were mounted on top of the toilet seat not under the seat as intended. Neither Mom nor Dad ever noticed. They had to be very uncomfortable sitting on the bar that went across the handles.

I REMEMBER (2/9/2012)

Ever since Christmas, Dad had been coming out with random statements about things he remembered.

Today I took him to the eye doctor for a routine checkup.

As had become the usual routine, Mom came and talked to everyone in the waiting room while I sat with Dad in the examination room. Waiting for the doctor, he started the conversation.

"Is it true this year I've been married to my wife for sixty-three years?

"Yes, in September."

"Jim sold the sailboat to a farmer, right?"

"You're right."

"If I remember, T.J., Jim's oldest grandson, is an Eagle Scout, and that's the highest you can go."

"Right again, Pop."

"And Katie, Jim's granddaughter, is she still doing gymnastics?"

"Yes, she is a very good gymnast."

He continued, "Isabella is a great tennis player, but I think Dante is the best of all." He smiled as he said, "That's because you told me he takes after me."

At that moment the doctor entered the room. For the first time in my life, I wanted a doctor to keep me waiting longer. I missed conversations with Dad and wished this one had been longer.

MISSING TOOTH (2/14/2012)

Happy Valentine's Day!

Today Mom and Dad had dental appointments to get their teeth cleaned. The rain was coming down heavily, so Jim offered to go with me. I called three times to make sure they were getting ready.

When I walked in, Mom was still on the bed with only her bra on. Dad was dressed and brushing his teeth. I helped Mom finish getting dressed, put the flowers I brought them in a vase, filled their pillboxes, and went to clean up the bathroom.

On the ride over to the dentist's office, Mom blurted out, "You know old people do crazy things."

"They most certainly do," I answered to myself.

Mom got her teeth cleaned first. When she returned to the waiting room she asked, "How much do they charge for cleaning?"

"The dentist charges eighty-five dollars," I responded.

She couldn't believe it. She announced very seriously, "Well, I have a missing tooth and should get credit for it.

Being a little silly I replied, "How many teeth do you have? I'll ask the hygienist to prorate the cleaning based on the number."

She proceeded to count her teeth using her tongue. Her eyes moved in sync with her tongue as she counted the bottom teeth on the right, and her eyes shifted to the left as she started counting the teeth on the left. She got confused a few times and started over again.

After counting the bottom, she started the same exercise on the top. Then she shouted, "I think twenty-seven teeth. Please tell the hygienist, so I can get a credit."

SO SMOOTH (2/22/2012)

Dad had been complaining about his shaving cream for a week. I had bought him both gel and foam shaving creams, not knowing which he preferred. When I asked if he was using the foam or gel, all he could say was, "I don't like it. It's not as good as the last stuff you bought me."

While visiting them today, I decided to look in the medicine cabinet to see what kind he was using. I almost fell over when I saw the can next to his razor – Pledge Lemon Fresh furniture polish.

I couldn't stop laughing. I didn't even attempt to figure out how he thought the polish, which I had left under the kitchen sink, was his shaving cream. We joked about how lemony fresh Dad's face was and laughed until it hurt.

Mom was the first to stop laughing. She went up to Dad put her hand on his cheek, and said, "Len, I love your smooth face, but how could you not have seen that it was furniture polish?"

"I don't shave with my glasses on, and I can't see."

Mom surprisingly remembered this all day and during our nightly conversation said she could not believe Dad would do such a dumb thing and started to laugh again.

SIBLING (2/27/2012)

My father's eighty-eight-year-old sister was not doing well. I asked Dad if he would like to talk to her. He nodded his head.

This was his only living sister, and she had been distressed thinking he had forgotten her. Mom and Dad ended phone communication with friends and relatives when his hearing diminished and when she could no longer carry on a conversation without repeating herself.

My aunt was now living with her daughter. I called my cousin and arranged a time for them to have a Skype video call.

They were happy to see each other, but had very little to say. My cousin and I tried to ask questions to get the conversation started, but had little success.

Dad did manage to share something of importance to him. "I love to dance, and I dance with Miss E when we have parties."

OVEREXPOSED (2/28/2012)

As I entered my parents' building, I could hear my name called. I turned around to greet the activities director.

After pleasant hellos, she mentioned that Mom could use some new blouses. She explained that on several recent occasions, she – the director - and my Dad would have to stand on opposite sides of my mother and pull down her blouse. If this task wasn't performed, Mom's blouse rode up and exposed two inches of her waist. Mom's extra weight combined with the shrinking of her cotton blouses in the dryer was the cause of this problem.

I immediately left for the mall to pick up as many blouses as I could find in my mother's size. All I could find were three, all the same shade of blue but with different patterns. This was fine, since Mom favored wearing blue.

I returned to my parents' apartment and cleared the closet of all shirts that no longer fit due to the dryer and Mom's weight gain.

Mom was thrilled with the blouses and I was thrilled the problem was solved so easily. She kept repeating, "How did you know blue was my favorite color?"

HAVE YOU BEEN HERE BEFORE? (3/11/2012)

Mom and Dad were still sitting in the dining room finishing lunch when Jim and I walked in. We went to their table to join them for a cup of coffee.

They greeted us with big hellos and smiles.

Mom started the conversation by asking us if we had ever been there before.

It was a gorgeous day, and I thought every azalea bush in Savannah was in full bloom. Jim and I decided it would be nice to get Mom and Dad out for a drive to show them the azaleas. When Mom and Dad got in the car, Jim convinced us that stopping for a small frozen yogurt would be a good treat. Mom needed no convincing. We enjoyed a fun afternoon.

When we returned to Mom and Dad's apartment, I rode up on the elevator with them. Dad thanked me for a "great day." Mom remembered nothing.

Her memory continued to get worse and I found it difficult to accept. I'm so glad Mom can't remember the person she has become, and still thinks she is the person she was. I also find it frustrating that she knows she can't remember. I fear what life to come will hold for her.

HALL WALKER (3/16/2012)

The phone had rung at eight this morning. Seeing the name on the phone display window, I knew I had a problem.

It was the manager of Savannah Seniors calling to report my Dad had been seen sauntering down the hall to the bathroom in his T-shirt and Depends. The only response that came to mind was, "I'm sorry." I promised to call my parents and check out what happened.

Mom answered the phone and declared, "The toilet is broken, and it won't flush. Water is on the floor and I have to go now. I need to crap."

I called the manager back and explained the problem. Later in the day the maintenance man notified me that he had found a piece of a Styrofoam plate lodged in the toilet. Neither one of my parents could explain how it got there.

Two days had passed since the toilet episode. When I questioned Dad on whether the carpet had dried, all he said was, "A little bit."

I decided to go over and checked it out. Walking by their bedroom, I would have been blind not to see the three-foot square water stain on their bedroom rug near the bathroom. The spot was soaking wet.

I called Maintenance and reported the problem.

MORE WATER (3/22/2012)

I stopped in to see Mom and Dad today. Neither one had mentioned the water problem in days, so I assumed it was fixed.

I asked the fellow at the front desk if the maintenance man ever determined what caused the water in my parents' apartment. He was hesitant to answer me. With some coaxing, I finally got an answer.

"The maintenance man thinks the water was urine."

"Urine?" I said. "I know my parents are old but the toilet is six inches from the wet spot. How could Dad's aim be that bad?"

As the minutes passed I was getting angrier and angrier with the maintenance man. I didn't want this rumor to roam the halls among the staff. That would become a clear path to assisted living.

I went back to my Mom and Dad's apartment. This time I got on my hands and knees seeing if I could find the origin of the leak. Using a paper towel, I touched every plastic pipe connected to the toilet. Finally success, the paper towel was wet revealing the origin of the leak. Admittedly, I soaked up the water on the carpet and put it to my nose for a test. I was relieved; it was not urine.

I went as fast as I could to the reception desk in search of the maintenance man. The receptionist informed me the maintenance man wanted to see me as well.

In no time he appeared behind me and started to explain he could not find a leak. Before he had a chance to complete his sentence, I blurted, "What do you see on this paper towel?"

"Uh, I see nothing."

"Would you mind smelling it?" I pushed the wad of wet paper towels toward his nose.

He replied, "I smell nothing."

"Right. It's not urine. If you come upstairs, I'll show you were the leak is."

We both got down on the floor as I pointed out where the water was dripping from.

He seemed puzzled and called the other maintenance man on duty.

I left pleased that my parents had not peed on the carpet, and that I had stopped the spread of any accusations that would have forced them into assisted living.

Days had passed since the water problems. I checked on my parents today. The carpet was not only dry but had been cleaned.

As I was leaving, the maintenance man was walking in my direction. He was looking down and avoiding eye contact. I wanted to know what caused the toilet problem, so I called out his name and said hello. I was happy to find out that it was a small leak in the water-line feeder that needed replacement. I was even happier to know he knew it wasn't my parents that caused the problem.

TIME TO GO (3/31/2012)

It took several years for Jim and me to sell our home, but today we received an offer. We were moving to Charleston to be closer to my grandchildren. My grandmother had been a large part of my life. She taught me to knit, crochet, and cook. Together we played countless games of Old Maid and Gin Rummy. Her love for me was unconditional as mine was for her. Years later my mother readily accepted her role as grandmother. I wanted my turn to be an involved grandma.

I knew it was also time to move my parents to assisted living. Moving them to the assisted living facility located on the same site as their current residence would have burdened them with the stress of knowing that was where their friends had gone to die. Having them move to an assisted living facility in Charleston came with no history or preconceived ideas. My parents would accept the decision readily, since we were all moving, but I dreaded the idea of assisted living.

CAN YOU HEAR ME NOW? (4/6/2012)

Dad's hearing had been getting progressively worse, especially in his left ear.

Today we went to get his hearing tested. A young, attractive, smiling audiologist greeted us. She led us into a very small testing room and hooked a device on both of Dad's ears. I explained his problem and mentioned several times that he was ninety-one. I'm not sure why I repeated Dad's age other than to emphasize that the solution needed to be uncomplicated.

The audiologist closed the door as she initiated the test from an adjoining room. She asked Dad to tell her when he could hear a beep. I could hear everything from my chair across from him. He heard very little.

Next she asked Dad to repeat the words she said. She started with, "Say the word *baseball.*"

Dad replied, "Baseball."

"Say the word *railroad.*"

Dad's reply was "Dante." I thought maybe I didn't hear him correctly. Dante was my grandson's name.

"Say the word *cowboy.*"

Dad again answered, "Dante."

"Say the word *red.*"

Dad replied, "Say the word *brown.*"

"Say the word *off.*"

Dad chimed in, "Say the word *cat.*"

The audiologist announced to Dad that she was finished with the testing, and helped him exit the room. She turned to me and said, "Your assessment is correct. Your Dad has severe loss in the left ear and moderate to severe in the right ear, depending on the pitch."

She guided us into an examination room to wait for the doctor.

The doctor spent a few minutes looking into Dad's ears. He pulled out dead skin from Dad's ears with awful-looking tweezers that made Dad wince with pain. He repeated the testing results talking about decibels, which brought a puzzled look on my father's face, and advised a hearing aid for Dad's right ear. I again communicated Dad was ninety-one and could no longer change a TV remote control battery, let alone a tiny hearing aid battery.

Then I asked my favorite "doctor question." "What would you do if this were your Dad?"

He paused. "Let me talk with the audiologist." He came back in a short time, and proposed a hearing aid with a rechargeable battery.

After the appointment, Dad asked me every day when was he going to get the "hearing thing."

THE SEARCH (4/12/2012)

The assisted-living search had begun. The Internet was my first point of reference, and I narrowed the search down to residences within ten miles of our new home. Checking on my parents would be easier if they lived close to us.

My criteria for an assisted living residence consisted of: a bright and sunny facility that did not smell of old age, smiling residents and staff, an enthusiastic activities director, good food, and, naturally, cost.

Jim and I visited several places, but upon arrival at Senior Plateau we knew this was my parents' new home. Walking up to the front door, smiling residents sitting in rocking chairs on the front porch greeted us. The rest of the visit only got better. The staff was friendly, the activities director amazing and the facility bright and clean. The best part was it was located one mile from our new home.

AUNT KATHY (4/23/2012)

Dad's youngest sister passed away today. I called this morning to let him know.

"Hi, Pop. I'm sorry to tell you that Aunt Kathy died this morning."

"You mean my sister Kathy?"

"Yes, Aunt Kathy in California."

"Oh, that's too bad."

"Sorry, Pop."

"Thank you."

That was the end of our conversation. He never asked how she died or anything else about his sister. I realized at his age, death was an everyday occurrence.

I CAN HEAR (4/24/2012)

Today Mom, Dad and I went to get Dad's hearing aid. He appeared to be anxious. Mom waited for us and passed the time complimenting every child in the waiting room on how handsome they were. Seven boys that appeared to be under the age of six were either waiting to see a doctor or with someone who was waiting.

Mom proclaimed, "Isn't it interesting those young boys are so cute? I don't think God makes funny-looking people anymore. I could not say that about children years ago. Some were not so cute."

Dad's fitting went well, and when we walked out Dad had a new perspective. He could now hear out of his right ear. It was wonderful.

I led Mom and Dad to the restrooms while I paid the bill. When I finished I returned to wait for them. Outside the restrooms was a woman whom I had noticed with her elderly mother in the waiting room. She turned to me and said, "I think we have the same job."

I knew exactly what she meant and replied, "I think we do."

She continued, "I lost my Dad a few months ago and now only care for my mom. I never imagined I would have to help my dad change his diaper, but I guess he changed plenty of mine."

How I could relate. I told her I understood completely and wished her well.

When we arrived back at Mom and Dad's apartment, I plugged the charging unit into an electric outlet in the bedroom, and placed it on Dad's night table.

I wrote instructions on what Dad needed to do at night and in the morning with his hearing aid. At night he had to place the hearing aid into the unit, and close the lid. In the morning he had to take the hearing aid out, press a small button on the device, and put it in his ear. I had him go through the process several times until I was comfortable that he could handle it alone.

The next morning I called to make sure Dad was using the hearing aid. Mom answered, and I could hear the TV blasting in the background. They had returned from chair aerobics.

"Hi, Mom. Is Pop using his hearing aid?"

"Ask him."

I could hear her handing Dad the phone.

"Hello?"

"Hi, Pop. Are you using the hearing aid?"

"What?"

I shouted my question a second time. This time he replied, "It's in my ear."

I found out later he had it in backwards.

ANOTHER BIRTHDAY (5/3/2012)

Today was my birthday. I knew my parents would not remember the day.

I was correct. When I called neither one remembered. I asked if they would like to have lunch with Jim and me. The invitation was readily accepted.

I had to remind Mom several times during lunch that it was my birthday. We had a pleasant time, and most importantly, they celebrated my birthday with me.

You would think that at sixty-one years old, my parents' not remembering my birthday shouldn't bother me, but it did. I was saddened but accepted the fact that they were not at fault.

SHAVING CREAM (5/11/2012)

Dad only called me when he needed something. Today it was shaving cream. I had recently bought him two cans.

When I called this morning Dad answered and informed me he needed shaving cream. Only three weeks had passed since I bought him the two cans.

This afternoon a message was on the answering machine. The voice was very familiar, "Mariann, I need shaving cream."

Tonight Dad called again to ask me to bring him more shaving cream when I got a chance. He must be eating it!

MISSING CLOTHES (6/12/2012)

During today's visit, I noticed my father only had one pair of pants in the closet, and Mom only had a couple of tops.

"Where are your clothes?"

They both looked at me, puzzled. "In the closet," Dad replied.

I walked down to the laundry room. I looked in both dryers and both washing machines. Empty. I plodded back to their apartment and searched again. No luck. Back to the laundry room I went for another look. When residents forgot to get their clothes out of the dryer, they would be stored in one of the cabinets. When I opened every cabinet, I had no luck. In their apartment again, I looked in the bathroom, front closet, and even under their bed. By now I was totally frustrated.

Something inside my head triggered me to go back to the laundry room. I opened the dryers and looked into the wash machines. I noticed at the very bottom of one machine were their clothes, laying flat and half dry.

How I missed this on my last two trips to the laundry room still concerns me. Was it stress or something else? Maybe I needed assisted living.

ASSISTED LIVING (6/22/2012)

More than four years had passed since Mom and Dad took that final picture in front of their old home in New Haven, Connecticut, and moved to Savannah.

Today Jim and I were moving them to Charleston. I had not shared with my parents that they would be moving into an assisted-living facility. I hoped they might not notice.

Jim and a friend loaded the rental truck with Mom and Dad's few remaining possessions. My parents patiently sat in the lobby, saying goodbye to their friends and staff members.

Dad gave his dance partner, Miss E a big hug and told her she would be missed.

Mom seemed confused each time she noticed a piece of furniture she recognized go out the door. When I reminded Mom that Jim and I would be living near them, the smile returned to her face.

When the truck was loaded, we were all ready for our next venture.

Mom and Dad walked out as they had walked in four years ago, trusting in me.

EPILOGUE

I've come to the conclusion my mother is too afraid to die, and Dad is too afraid to leave her alone.

If my parents can continue to live with dignity and without pain, I hope they live forever.

I have seen too many people living a non-existent life in nursing homes and pray every day that God takes my parents quickly and without pain.

I don't know what the future holds for my parents, and sometimes fear the road ahead. I do know I will try my best to continue to see them not as the people they have become, but as the people they were.

I will look at them and remember the strong, loving, and caring people who were part of the Greatest Generation. They were parents who put family first and taught me values I will always cherish: devotion and love of God and family, respect and kindness to all, and forgiveness – because life is too precious for grudges.

I want to remember my mother as the smiling, friendly, young, pretty girl in the red coat that my Dad fell in love with, and Dad as the handsome, proud Marine who loves to dance.

I will continue to write to relieve my stress, and only God knows for how much longer.

Who are these people? They are your parents, your relatives, your friends, your neighbors, and someday yourself. They are people we love.

35333644R00134

Made in the USA
Charleston, SC
05 November 2014